The Recovery of Joy

The Bible Reading Fellowship
15 The Chambers, Vineyard
Abingdon OX14 3FE
brf.org.uk

The Bible Reading Fellowship (BRF) is a Registered Charity (233280)

ISBN 978 0 85746 518 4
First published 2017
10 9 8 7 6 5 4 3 2 1 0

Acknowledgements
Scripture quotations are taken from The Holy Bible, New International Version
(Anglicised edition) copyright © 1979, 1984, 2011 by Biblica. Used by permission of
Hodder & Stoughton Publishers, an Hachette UK company. All rights reserved.
'NIV' is a registered trademark of Biblica. UK trademark number 1448790

Every effort has been made to trace and contact copyright owners for material used
in this resource. We apologise for any inadvertent omissions or errors, and would
ask those concerned to contact us so that full acknowledgement can be made in
the future.

A catalogue record for this book is available from the British Library

Printed and bound by CPI Group (UK) Ltd, Croydon CR0 4YY

The Recovery of Joy

Finding the
path from rootlessness
to returning home

Naomi Starkey

This book was a long time in development, so thanks to all who listened to me, supported me and helped me clarify what I wanted to say. Special thanks to Richard J., who gave me the idea of 'islands', without which the narrative would never have reached its final shape.

Contents

Introduction

To be a pilgrim is commonly assumed to have some sense of purpose. To be a pilgrim usually means setting off, after due planning and provision, careful forecasting and budgeting. To be a pilgrim means anticipating some kind of holy encounter, if not along the way – and possibly not through our fellow pilgrims – then certainly when we reach our destination, the sacred, thin place that is reputed to be a likely spot for connecting with God. And to be a pilgrim means setting off in the happy confidence that home awaits our return.

In a number of spiritual traditions, both Christianity and other faiths, there has also been another kind of pilgrim, more of a wanderer than a traveller, a seeker rather than one who is intent on a particular destination. Celtic monks of the fifth and sixth centuries sometimes chose such wandering as a form of martyrdom, in the absence of active persecution. They would literally push off (so the stories tell) from the shore in tiny boats, oar-less, and trust to heaven's mercy to direct their way over the water. And (so the stories tell) heaven was usually gracious and brought them through mishap and adventure to a place of final rest. Theirs was a different, reckless purpose, abandoning themselves to God's purposes, as mediated through wind and current and tide. They did not ask to see a map; they did not worry about losing the way, because they had moved beyond the notion of 'lost'.

Then again, some may set out on a journey, not as a kind of martyrdom, nor even as purposeful travellers, but as those who are going into exile. They leave behind pretty much everything known as home – through choice, through force of circumstance, whatever – and then just carry on, taking a turning here, a sidetrack there, simply to do something. Movement is one of the signs of life – and so they move and keep on moving, empty of purpose, empty of agenda or timetable, perhaps empty even of the search for any kind of meaning. Keeping going, even if mechanically, even if randomly and pointlessly, can keep you one step ahead of remorse, recrimination, regret, and one step can be enough.

Such a journey is not a pilgrimage but it can become one. This book shares a story of exile and rootless wandering that, through unlooked-for grace, finds purpose and becomes pilgrimage. Starting at a point where purpose has collapsed to a point of near-paralysis, a wanderer chooses to drift across a sea in a small boat that unexpectedly turns out to be a vessel of salvation, of redemption. This sea hides islands, those little worlds so beloved of pilgrims and travellers of every kind because they apparently offer safety and seclusion from the trials and complexities of the rest of life. Appearances are only part of the truth, however, as we shall discover.

The islands that we will discover in this book turn out to be places of encounter, challenge and eventual transformation. Brokenness is stitched together, painfully, to make a new, beautiful whole. The conclusive discovery is realising the way to the recovery of joy – that transfiguring sense of wholeness, rootedness, delight and peace that can catch us unawares, breaking through a seemingly chance convergence of time, place and self, and calling us to respond. The way to that recovery, that joy, emerges as we find ourselves caught up in the creator's working. It comes to clarity through knowing, beyond doubt, that this here and now is the only place we should be, what we were born for. However far we fall, we cannot fall beyond the reach of God's loving arms if we shout for rescue. We cannot run so far or so long that his loving gaze will cease scanning the horizon in the hope of glimpsing our return.

As the events of the story unfold, each chapter will pause for reflection on selected passages from the Psalms, the ancient prayer book of God's people. The Psalms are one of the parts of scripture that most reverberate with human passions – despair, longing, hope, joy – as the people who first composed those prayers struggled to hold together their belief in God's loving providence with the strains of living in a baffling and at times frightening world. Almost without exception, they found renewed assurance by the closing verses. Like a flashlight on the darkest and stormiest of nights, the central message of the Psalms lights up a trustworthy path to follow: 'This is not the end that it seems. Don't give up. God is here – promise.'

Part 1

Rootlessness

1

On the road

Here we are at a crossroads once again. Here we are, standing in a thin drizzle under a grey sky, staring at a white fingerpost pointing in four different directions to places that mean nothing to us.

How did we end up here – and which way to go now?

It had seemed a good idea at first – throwing away the rule book of a good life, tearing up the old maps. It felt adventurous, a more sophisticated way of carrying on than dutifully following the ways trodden by parents, grandparents, mentors, vicars, teachers, the law-abiding and unremittingly respectable. We were going to strike out on our own, break new ground, making a better, more free and authentic way for ourselves, a way that would bring fulfilment, excitement, gloriously boosted self-esteem. Choices were made, ultimatums delivered, promises broken, and then somehow or other it all turned into the most horrible mess. Instead of ascending the heights, we have found ourselves falling into a pit – a pit of our own digging.

And now we find ourselves here, wandering an apparently endless maze of small, muddy lanes. They are no doubt attractive to jaded city-dwellers visiting on a sunny day, but under this grey sky, the drizzle driven against the face by the fretful wind, they sap the soul's energy. When we started off, longer ago than we care to remember, we found a virtue in taking the alternative route, the one that none of our friends was following. We always assumed there would be a route back (a shortcut, if possible) to life's highway, where we would rejoin the rest of the traffic, pick up on relationships temporarily suspended, get back to normal (albeit a different kind of normal).

Sure, we had fun along the way, some unplanned stopovers and unexpected discoveries, while the rest of the traffic filed dutifully along the dual carriageway, nose to tail. We have a truckload of entertaining anecdotes to share, which show us in the best possible light, despite the arguable un-wisdom of our choices. Now, though, we don't have anybody to share them with. We are utterly alone and have been for some time.

Even yesterday, we could still tell ourselves that the only way is forward, that tomorrow is another day – and while there is life, there is hope. And so on. Now, today, that feels like ridiculous optimism.

Until today we still hoped that the sun would break through the clouds. We hoped that the wind would drop, that (getting desperate) a voice would thunder from the skies and tell us which direction to take. Some say that an instinct of the heart kicks in to let us know the right path to take – that we sense a welling up of dread if we are about to go the wrong way, or a sudden flood of peace if we are making a good choice – but what does a pervasive numbness of the heart signify? How do we cope with a growing paralysis of will that begins to make every direction look to be leading to the wrong destination? The trouble is (or part of the trouble is) that we are so far from home, so removed from all familiar landmarks.

We are lost.

For a while we pretended that we were on a kind of pilgrimage – but we were fooling ourselves. We have not been seeking divine connection (quite the opposite, in fact); neither have we been consciously heading in search of some place or other where the cosmic 'heavenly dimension' is said to be particularly accessible. We have lacked fellow pilgrims to support us with tea and sympathy when the journey grew burdensome. Now we have no one around to remind us not to worry, that God is bigger than we know... and so on.

What we have been doing was not pilgrimage, but just aimless wandering – and, today, wandering in circles. And now we are lost.

The thin drizzle is turning into solid rods of rain and the pointy tops of the surrounding hills have disappeared into a blanket of fog. And so it's both a surprise and a relief when a muddy pickup truck pulls up alongside, towing a trailer full of sheep. The window winds down and a smiling wind-beaten face suggests that we might like a lift as it looks as if we are heading down the same road... and the weather is dismal, isn't it?

The kindness of strangers can be heartbreaking, offered (as it can be) without obligation, and with casual generosity. It's probably best not to disintegrate at this point, though. Who knows what further emotional assault course lies ahead for us?

But we can accept a lift and climb in, as crumpled government forms, empty crisp packets, chocolate wrappers and a copy of last week's local newspaper (folded open at the classified ads for livestock) are knocked off the front seat. The radio offers wry commentary on celebrity entanglements that sound like dispatches from another universe.

Some claim to have received heaven's guidance through a random song popping up on a DJ's playlist, or in a passing comment on a TV show that includes exactly the words or image needed to direct their decision-making. An omnipotent God can surely manipulate media chat to deliver appropriate help for his hapless children, yet then the challenge is to know where guidance ends and delusion takes over. Maybe the truth is found in the outcome – whether the apparent guidance produces sound or sour fruit in the lives of those affected. It's all rather hypothetical for us, though, in the utter absence of any such help, any guidance as to where to go next.

Thankfully, our driver seems happy to carry on mostly in easy silence, offering a few comments on the rain and the road but a merciful lack of probing questions. Given that we have no destination in mind, given that we are lost (in every sense of the word), it is a relief to be rattled along for a while, delaying the moment when the next choice becomes unavoidable. Our desperate state must be fairly obvious, though, as the next comment indicates:

'If you're planning to sleep out tonight, the forecast isn't good. If you're going to walk the cliffs, the wind will cut straight through that coat. But if you want a place to stop over, just till the morning, we have spare beds and space at the supper table.'

Just for a moment a door swings open into a parallel world – a world of firelight, food and conviviality, a family circle extended wide enough to include the lost and straying. Just for a moment, we wonder if we could step through that door. We hesitate, with all the irresolution that has been our habit for so long, and the moment slips past.

'This is the turning to my place here – so…?'

So – thanks, but no thanks. The rain has stopped, for now.

As has become our routine of late, not deciding has led to a decision. We will not take the turning; we will walk away from the spare bed, the place at the table. We will walk on into the low grey afternoon and we will despair.

I am laid low in the dust; preserve my life according to your word.
I gave an account of my ways and you answered me; teach me
    your decrees.
Cause me to understand the way of your precepts,

that I may meditate on your wonderful deeds.
My soul is weary with sorrow; strengthen me according to your
  word.
Keep me from deceitful ways; be gracious to me and teach me
  your law.
I have chosen the way of faithfulness; I have set my heart on your
  laws.
I hold fast to your statutes, Lord; do not let me be put to shame.
I run in the path of your commands, for you have broadened my
  understanding.
Teach me, Lord, the way of your decrees, that I may follow it to the
  end.
Give me understanding, so that I may keep your law and obey it
  with all my heart.
Direct me in the path of your commands, for there I find delight.
Turn my heart towards your statutes and not towards selfish gain.
PSALM 119:25–36

This is the voice of one clinging to God by the fingertips, as life events crash on top of them, crushing them face down in the dirt. This is the voice of one who has tried to walk God's way, the way of faithfulness, but found it did not deliver what had been hoped. After all, the scriptures abound in promises of fullness of life and overflowing granaries for the righteous, blessings for those who commit themselves, body and soul, to following the law. We may ask, then, why this upright and blameless speaker has been left grovelling in the dust. Since when has that been part of the life script for those seeking to be obedient sons and daughters of the Most High?

What we also hear, however, is the dogged determination not to let go of God, imploring his help to ensure that no error in the speaker's life, even the most innocent of mistakes, is overlooked. 'Keep me from deceitful ways,' is the plea. 'Be gracious to me, don't let me be put to shame. Strengthen me, direct me, teach me.' Oh God, please don't leave me here in bits… I long to long for you, and you alone, with all my heart – but I fear my own weakness, my regrettable tendency to deceive even myself. I am so easily trapped by my small and selfish desires. Without you, O God, I can only crawl forward, a pathetic specimen. With you, O God, I have the confidence and strength to rise to my feet and not just walk, but run freely along the broad and blessed path of obedience, the path that I know to be the path of life.

Please hear me. Please help me.

We might want to critique such a perspective as infantilising. Surely, as adults, we are supposed to make up our own minds about where to go and how to get there, whether we're talking about what career to pursue, what person to marry – or what car to buy or how to spend our day off. We don't need downloaded route plans, no matter how sanctified and scriptural, because surely we have made enough journeys by now to have a pretty good idea of possible outcomes. Pity the poor religious obsessive who cannot take a step forward without the say-so of the big Santa in the sky…

But what about the times when our choices – whether carefully weighed decisions or momentary and perhaps regrettable impulses – take us into a maze of uncertainty where the only exit leads to what feels like the very end of the road? In these verses we hear the near-despair of one gripping with fading strength to the statutes of God as their last chance of guidance, of a sense of perspective, a means of orientation in the dizzy confusion of what to do. Note, however, that faith somehow turns that near-despair to an impulse of hope. God is good – that is a given – and God's way is good – another given – and so when God reveals to us the right way to go, we can walk on in trust.

And whatever helps us on the journey from despair to hope can only be beneficial for the soul, whether or not we find it easy to admit the finitude of our personal resources, and bring ourselves to ask for help; whether or not we choose to walk with God or to wander away altogether.

The afternoon light gets lower and greyer by the minute as we trudge the narrowing lanes, although by now it's more of a shuffle than anything so determined as a trudge. Our feet are hurting badly. These lanes are only the width of an average car now… perhaps in another turning or two we will come to the end.

What then?

It's easier not to ask that. It's easier just to trudge – to shuffle on – because when the days are as empty as ours have become, movement brings a crumb of meaning. As we breathe, as we move, we know that time is passing which is, in a way, a good thing. Time passing will bring closer the final ending of all choice, the conclusive shutting down of options, and that will come as a relief, to be honest. We have had enough.

2

Dead end

Well, of all the possible scenarios, we have managed to select the worst, as usual. We have come to the end of the road, brought there by the failure to choose that ends up being a choice after all. But we have not reached a proud cliff face towering above a poetic, pounding sea, nor sun-kissed sand dunes leading down to a gentle shore. We have ended up floundering in epic mud, claggy clay soil slick with yesterday's bad weather, which threatens to scoot us over the edge where the land slithers on to the beach in lumps of fallen rock and tufts of grass. At our back, there is a derelict campsite, battered to bits by last winter's gales. Just below, in the low, grey light, we can see scraps of fibreglass and metal smeared down the slope, with the occasional scrap of beige upholstery snagged on the thorny weeds – the ghost of a caravan.

As we are too exhausted to go back (and there is nothing to return to, anyway), and unable to go further, the only option is standing and looking at the mess. This is what we have come to – this grubby, pathetic ending.

And soon darkness will be falling.

Standing here, if we lift our eyes, we see the sea, which can so often move the heart with expansive blue horizons, hinting at alternative scenarios and possible adventures (if we are bold enough to dare). Here and now, though, if we look up and out, we see ominous layers of cloud piled in the west, murky against the murky waters, and threatening to roll closer, fast, on the blustery wind. Remembered words reverberate unhelpfully: 'If you're planning to sleep out tonight, the forecast is not good.'

As the clouds and darkness build ahead of us, now is the time for retrieving from the back of the mind the Plan B that – surely – we must have stored up for such a moment. Surely we had thought of (if only to lay aside) an escape route, a handful of possibilities to sustain us in life's unforeseen unravelling (such as this messy, muddy edge). This endpoint – no way forward, no way back – means we are cornered at last, forced beyond denial to see what a complete shambles we have made of our freedom to choose. We have overlooked completely the consequences of wandering. Stupidly, we had assumed that securities (financial, material, emotional) would always be there as a fallback if our wandering life failed to work out as hoped, if we found ourselves wanting to come home again, metaphorical tail between metaphorical legs, adventures over and done with. But here we are, stupidly stuck, humiliated.

We remember the offer of a bed, of food – but what chance of finding our way back along the maze of lanes and locating that haven now, in the gathering twilight?

Then we feel raindrops again; we have left it too late. We have hesitated and we have lost – and even faster than we feared, the weather worsens. The rain is thickening and now it lashes us, drenches us, and then turns to hail, flung in our faces by furious atmospheric turbulence. Flinching, blinking, stumbling away from the muddy edge, we surely look a pitiful sight, except that there is nobody left to have pity on us, nobody to care, to reach out and draw us back to warmth and light and safety.

With painful relevance, words of a long-ago wise man come to mind: we have sown the wind – and now we reap the whirlwind. And whirlwinds have a habit of ripping away the last remnants of security, the flimsy roof that we have patched once too often to try and cope with another winter (instead of asking ourselves why life feels like one endless winter), the scanty curtains that were just about adequate to preserve modesty – all gone in a moment.

As the full force of the wind hits us, so does a realisation – one that we have been fending off for a very long time. The truth is finally undeniable: we can blame no one for this outcome but ourselves. We took those choices, we walked those paths, and we rejected offers of help and shelter because we still felt a bit invincible, still proud enough and strong enough to say no, in the expectation that something better would turn up.

Stupid, stupid, stupid.

The rain has easily penetrated our feeble layers of clothing and the wind is snatching away body heat fast. There is no mercy in this weather, in this place. We could be finished off before the storm has blown itself out – but not here, please. It would be better to crawl away somewhere we can't be found, rather than simply curling up on the path, to be discovered hours or days later like a bundle of cast-off clothes, and making the headlines in the local newspapers. Better to disappear altogether, in the hope of retaining a small rag of dignity.

Then, for a breath or two, the wind drops slightly. For a breath or two, the darkness lifts a little, just enough to hint that there might be a way down to the beach after all – there, to the left of the wrecked caravan. What looked like a stream-bed could also be a sort of path. Dangerously steep, by the looks of it, but the shore does not look so very far below.

Who knows but that this may be our final choice? As every other of our choices has proved to have disastrous consequences (or so it feels right now), if this ends up disastrously – well, that will not trouble us.

We start to clamber down, as best we can in the wind and rain, and sooner than we expect, we reach the bottom and stand, shakily, on sand and stone.

Lord, you are the God who saves me; day and night I cry out to you.
May my prayer come before you; turn your ear to my cry.
I am overwhelmed with troubles and my life draws near to death.
I am counted among those who go down to the pit; I am like one
*   without strength.*
I am set apart with the dead, like the slain who lie in the grave,
whom you remember no more, who are cut off from your care.
You have put me in the lowest pit, in the darkest depths.
Your wrath lies heavily on me; you have overwhelmed me with all
*   your waves.*
You have taken from me my closest friends and have made me
*   repulsive to them.*
I am confined and cannot escape; my eyes are dim with grief…
From my youth I have suffered and been close to death;
I have borne your terrors and am in despair.
Your wrath has swept over me; your terrors have destroyed me.
All day long they surround me like a flood; they have completely
*   engulfed me.*
You have taken from me friend and neighbour – darkness is my
*   closest friend.*

PSALM 88:1–9; 15–18

Here is a cry for help that is not answered even by the end of the psalm. The Lord God is implored with eloquent descriptions of desolation – the one doing the imploring feels as good as dead, swept away by a tsunami of troubles which (horrifyingly) have come from the hand of God himself. We are not told what has gone wrong, whether the troubles came through the speaker's wrongdoing or wrongdoings by others, but we are shown the consequences vividly.

The great fear voiced here is that the Lord has forgotten the victim. In the days when the Psalms were written, no concept had yet developed of life after the grave, the idea as yet unknown that death was a doorway to God's presence. To descend to 'the pit' was not to await resurrection but to be 'cut off' from the creator's sustaining love and care – and, says the speaker, that is how they feel right now. They have been abandoned not only by kin and community, but by the giver of life. Hope has gone, obliterated by the flood of divine anger that has surged (so the speaker says) the whole of their adult life.

Why, Lord?

No answer.

Why, Lord?

Still no answer.

But, the desolate one cries, I know you as the 'God who saves me'. Have you forgotten that that is who you are? You have taken everything from me (and let's not quibble for now as to whether this was deserved or not). Even those I counted as my friends now look on me with contempt. Have you not done enough to inflict hurt on me?

Yet again, no answer is forthcoming. The Lord who revealed himself to Moses as essential being, 'I am who I am' (Exodus 3:14), as quintessentially in covenant relationship with his chosen people ('the God of your father, the God of Abraham, the God of Isaac and the God of Jacob', v. 6) – the Lord God Almighty is silent.

So, the desolate one cries, I have truly lost everything that made life meaningful – and you, O God, seem indifferent to my plight. You have left me with no choice but to embrace the darkness of uncreation, the original void before there ever was light. That empty darkness is now more friend to me than you, O God. What do you say to that?

Silence.

Is that truly the end of hope, then? Not quite – because even as darkness is embraced, bitterly, as the last companion, the speaker knows that the One who brought light out of darkness in the very beginning is still there, somewhere, behind the clouds, beyond the storm. That is why they have spoken, that is why they have cried out – because they know that God is there. God seems indifferent to their plight, but the sense of indifference nevertheless implies belief in a presence to be indifferent. And, who knows, one day the floodwaters may recede, the clouds may part, and light may come again.

Maybe…

Down here on the stony, sandy shore, the day has faded so fast that we can see no more than vague, looming shapes. While the cliff was pretty much entirely mud, down here we find tumbled rocks, some smooth, others harsh to the touch as we grope our way forward. The rain is hammering on head and shoulders and soon indicates unsparingly the inadequacy of our footwear's waterproofing.

Everything is sodden.

Only one final effort is required of us, a last attempt to find a hiding place where we can embrace darkness as a strange kind of friend. Look, here: this patch of greater darkness proves to be a cave entrance. It's only a small cave but well above the high-tide line of dried seaweed. There's room to crawl inside and curl up; it's a little uncomfortable but tolerable enough. We close our eyes and let our last thought be the wish not to wake up again.

Surprisingly, sleep comes fast, as if the body senses that this hollow in the rocks is a safe space, and so suddenly lets go of consciousness.

And in the middle of night, when the darkness is deepest, here in this sea-smelling cave, dreams come so that for a time we return to scenes of peace and happiness – sunlight on newly mown grass, a cat curled up before a glowing wood stove, a little girl laughing on her birthday morning, a table spread for Sunday lunch with the family. Momentarily, we forget all that has been broken (that we have broken), perhaps beyond repair, and are lulled to deeper rest.

3

The pathless way

With a heavy heart, we open our eyes – and feel pain. There is a crick in our neck and our ribs have been bruised by an angle of rock. We are in pain and we are terribly hungry, the gnawing hollowness within indicating the many hours since we last ate properly. We can just about shuffle out of the cave the way we crawled in, when darkness fell last night. We had laid ourselves to rest, hoping never to wake again, but now we emerge from our rocky hideaway into a new day. We find ourselves blinking and stretching in a cold wind and we see the waves approaching purposefully up the beach. The tide is rising; the sun has not yet risen, but the eastern sky above the cliffs is growing lighter.

Good morning, world, so here we are again. Somewhat to our surprise (and disappointment), we have continued to breathe, our hearts to beat, our nervous systems to operate as usual. Waking to this new day does not feel like much of an achievement, though; nothing in our circumstances has changed.

We're starving hungry.

There's money in our pocket (damp) but where can we go to find food? At that thought, at the prospect of embarking again on the tedious progression of choice upon choice, we feel ourselves collapsing. The cave is still there – perhaps it would be easier to retreat, to shuffle back inside and curl up again, hoping for oblivion.

Then there, along the beach – how did we not see him before? – we catch sight of a man, kneeling, building a fire from a heap of driftwood, a black Labrador watching him. The flames are brisk and bright yellow, newly kindled, and as the man sits back on his heels, he glances over casually, as if he knew we were there, watching.

'Want to join me for some breakfast?'

Yes. Please.

Breakfast is simple but surprisingly plentiful – from somewhere or other, marmalade rolls appear, enough to satisfy even the appetite of those who can't remember their last proper meal. Good, strong coffee is poured from an apparently bottomless flask. We eat, we drink, and we sit side by side with our host, as the fire subsides to a warming bed of charcoal. The sun has risen properly now and in the clear light the sea looks invitingly blue.

'I wouldn't recommend a swim, though,' says our host, as if reading our thoughts. 'Not in this wind.' He rubs the ears of the Labrador and the dog thumps its tail happily.

In the far distance, obscured by early morning haze, we can just about glimpse dark smudges between sea and sky. Clouds?

'Islands,' says the man, as if reading our thoughts again. 'Worth a trip if you have the time. There are some fascinating places to explore out there.'

When life has reached a dead end such as ours, time is not a pressing issue.

'If you're interested' – he gestures to his right – 'you could borrow that… have a paddle around the bay.' A kayak is pulled up on the sand, the waves nudging beneath the stern, paddle resting on the hull, buoyancy aid propped against the back rest.

A pause – which turns into a surprisingly comfortable silence, seeing as we met this man less than an hour ago. The Labrador gets to its feet, nudges its master, looking hopefully at the remaining pile of sticks.

The man smiles at his dog and at us. 'Do you want to hear a story? It won't take long – and it gives you a bit more time to think about my offer.' Taking a slight tilt of the head for agreement, he begins, 'Once, long, long ago, a group of men came to this very beach. They weren't so confident on water but they had a plan in mind – and they were determined to see it through. And that determination was enough to overcome any lurking fears. What they were planning, you see, was to launch themselves in three little boats to see where the sea currents would take them. They hoped to make landfall somewhere before their food and water ran out, and before a storm blew up big enough to capsize them.

'Some of the locals gathered to watch them set off, shaking their heads and muttering that they'd never be seen again. They called them crazy and warned their children against even thinking of following their example. But you know what happened?'

No.

'Months passed, nearly a year. One day, a young boy was down on the beach, alone. And he looked up and there was a little boat drifting in to shore, which turned out to be one of those three little boats that had disappeared into the blue so long before. It was carrying just one man. He was burned dark brown by the sun, beard grown down to his chest, clothes faded into rags. His voice was hoarse with thirst but his face was shining with the memories of what he had seen and he would not stop talking, talking, talking, to the boy and then to everyone who came running to see this marvel.

'He had left his friends, so he said, on a beautiful, faraway island, full of waterfalls and hidden valleys and lush green leaves. He said that he had only returned to spread the word of what lay out there. He said that any who wanted could come back with him in the little boat, that the rewards far outweighed the risks. His legs proved too stiff for walking so he agreed, finally, to let the people carry him back to the nearby village so that he could rest and recover his strength for a day or so. He lay down on a soft bed, closed his eyes – and never opened them again, worn out by his adventures.

'When the fuss was over, the boy found and kept the little boat in a secret place, and sometimes he would look at it and remember the man's words. Although he never trusted himself to the sea currents, neither could he forget what he had heard. And every now and then, he would walk the beach early in the morning, walk and scan the horizon – and wonder.'

Give thanks to the Lord, for he is good; his love endures for ever.
Let the redeemed of the Lord tell their story –
those he redeemed from the hand of the foe, those he gathered
from the lands,
from east and west, from north and south…
Some went out on the sea in ships; they were merchants on the
mighty waters.
They saw the works of the Lord, his wonderful deeds in the deep.
For he spoke and stirred up a tempest that lifted high the waves.
They mounted up to the heavens and went down to the depths;
in their peril their courage melted away.
They reeled and staggered like drunkards; they were at their wits'
end.
Then they cried out to the Lord in their trouble, and he brought
them out of their distress.
He stilled the storm to a whisper; the waves of the sea were
hushed.
They were glad when it grew calm, and he guided them to their

> *desired haven.*
> *Let them give thanks to the Lord for his unfailing love and his*
>   *wonderful deeds for mankind.*
>
> PSALM 107:1–3, 23–31

The people of ancient Israel were not seasoned seafarers. They left that kind of thing to their neighbours on the Mediterranean coast and prided themselves on worshipping the one true God who, according to their scriptures, was in the habit of calming stormy waters and bringing forth dry land from the deep. The psalmist here speaks of the Lord 'stirring up a tempest' and then 'stilling the storm', showing his mastery of creation and evoking the appropriate response from his people: they 'cry out in their trouble' – and the Lord delivers them – and now they 'give thanks for his unfailing love' because, thanks to his guidance, they have reached their 'desired haven'.

Before the development of accurate navigation and weather forecasting instruments, sea travel was a high-risk affair – and those whose livelihood depended on it (merchants, fishermen) would have had a particularly healthy respect for the waywardness of wind and wave. They would have drawn on all their skill and wisdom to plan their ventures but, at the end of the day, they would have had to remember that reliance on the Lord was also essential. The monastic wanderers of later centuries, who literally cast themselves adrift on the ocean, trusting in God's providential care, were enacting something of this pattern (albeit in extreme form).

Such reliance is easy to forget when we feel able to pride ourselves on superior technology, long-range forecasting, and pinpoint accuracy. We map out our lives, predict the outcomes and are then outraged when life (being real) does not fit our plans. We manage to forget that we are not omnipotent and cannot hope to be omniscient – and that, one day, whether we like it or not, our little lives will come to an end. We forget that, if we know ourselves as 'the redeemed of the Lord', we should lay our plans and schemes within the context of his endless love and eternal purposes. Everything else is as futile as the chasing after the wind that the Preacher lamented (Ecclesiastes 2:17).

Sometimes, though, we are forcibly confronted with the futility when our choices go awry, when accidents happen, when we feel trapped in a spiral of catastrophe. What then? We may persist, painfully, in denial, hoping that we can blag our way out of the mess, somehow save the day – or we can admit defeat, reluctantly or with relief: 'I'm sorry. It's all gone wrong. Help me.' Then, as we see again and again throughout scripture, the Lord hears; the Lord comes; the Lord rescues.

It is a truth we do well to remember: God is beyond our limited spheres of space and time and yet entered and redeemed those spheres in the person of Jesus. We are not puppets of a scheming onlooker above the clouds; we are beloved children of the heavenly Father, who created us to grow to maturity. And in that process of growing, we should be mindful of our limits and our frail humanity.

'Go on – you can have a turn. You'll be fine. I'll see you again.'

The man's voice lingers, but when we look up, he is gone, and the Labrador too. The fire smoulders; the kayak lies waiting on the beach. It's not a sensible option (don't try this at home, kids) but here and now, we feel strangely exhilarated. We have nothing to lose. We think of the worst that could happen – drowning? – and right now that doesn't seem so very bad.

He told us to go on… and so, a few hours later, we do just that, pushing out on the ebbing tide. As we venture out from the bay, a current catches us and, with minimal effort, we find ourselves moving further and further from the shore. We have cast ourselves adrift – and right now, that feels a relief. We have been caught by the energies of something hugely bigger than our own fretting and angst and despair. At the very point where we had reached road's end, we have found a means of starting (or is it continuing?) a journey.

And there is evening.

And there is morning.

Part 2

Respite

4

Green pastures

It is very cold, bone-chillingly cold, out at sea just before sunrise. And it is probably even colder than usual because fog has shrunk the world to a small space of water, a white-walled floating cell round the kayak. Moisture coats every surface; the small sound of wavelet against hull is muffled. There is no sensation of movement – but fingers trailed in the water reveal that the current is still flowing. We are still being carried on, further from the shore, further out on to the deep.

It might be this coming of another new day that makes the heart start to thud with panic. Have we truly gone too far this time? There is no easy way back, even if we knew which way to go. Perhaps this current will continue to carry us remorselessly to the very end, wherever and whatever that is, whether we want it or not.

The panic and the pervading cold combine to prompt us to action. We retrieve the paddle from its stowing-place and start to work, pulling hard through the water. It's a struggle at first until we get the sense of working with, rather than against, the sea's energy, and our stiffened muscles begin to ease. The movement, the exercise, feels good, a reminder that the body can still function reasonably well, even if there is not much spirit left.

There's no way of measuring how much time passes, except to note that eventually even relatively strong arms start to tire. And – here's a thought – exertion creates thirst and the on-board water supply consists of a single two-litre bottle. That kind stranger had only encouraged us into the bay and we have gone far further than we imagined possible. Those smudges of island had not looked so far away. Have we (yet again) been going round in circles?

Meanwhile, the light is changing. The fog is starting to lift, to thin and to turn blue and gold as sky and sun emerge. The white, muffling walls are dispersing and then, hazy at first but growing clearer by the minute, we see that there is land ahead.

An island.

Panic starts to fade – and curiosity stirs. An island – why not explore? It's not as if the diary's crammed with appointments. Not that there is a diary any more. Perhaps we'll find a freshwater stream, something to refresh the bottle, enough for a little longer. But (the thought stirs in a dark recess of the heart) perhaps only a little longer will be necessary. That thought, to our surprise, jolts us in an uneasy kind of way. Maybe we are not ready for the end just yet.

The current looks set to carry the kayak past the island, but a few swift strokes of the paddle are enough to change trajectory. It's a small island of low green hills – three or four – that slope gently to the shore. Coming closer reveals that the nearest shoulder of land is divided, curving inwards to form a naturally sheltered harbour, a stretch of pleasingly golden sand dotted with pebbles. Digging in again with the paddle brings us gliding into the shallows, passing over a rock or two that loom up ominously through the clear water and waving columns of seaweed.

At last we can crunch ashore. Stepping out, our legs wobble after the long hours afloat, and the ground feels as if it is heaving beneath us. It's time to sit in a collapsed sort of way and let the glow of the newly minted sun begin to dry us out.

After a while, the urge to stretch cramped limbs propels us to scramble to our feet and start to take the measure of the place. We venture along the shoreline, through a tangle of the usual plastic flotsam, and round to another, wider bay that opens beyond our little harbour.

Then, quite improbably, we hear music.

Even more improbably, it's the jangling, all but irresistibly catchy sound of a honky-tonk piano, thumped out with (thankfully) equal measures of enthusiasm and musicality. Even though such music is not to our taste, it's hard not to smile at its unashamedly crowd-pleasing rhythm. This is not music to commit suicide to.

To smile after so long feels almost foolish, like striking a match on the off-chance that the wind won't blow it out immediately. It's a small, circumspect risk – and, having taken it, we imagine that we might take it again sometime in the not too distant future.

A half-dozen or so further steps along the bay, and the music's source comes into view – a whitewashed stone cottage nestled in a hollow of the green hill. The door stands open, and chords and melody spill down the grassy slope towards us. For a moment the whole situation feels disturbingly surreal, but even as we hesitate to go any closer, the music clatters to a halt and a voice booms out, 'You, down there – don't be a stranger! Come and say hello and have a cuppa!' And the pianist appears in the doorway – fills the doorway – her hands on her hefty hips, her grin widening like daybreak, white hair shining in the light.

'Be my guest!' she says – bellows, in fact – but her face radiates good humour and the force of her presence surges round her like a spring tide. Following her across the threshold leads us into a comfortable, cluttered room – upright piano (hammers exposed in proper honky-tonk style, of course), a round table covered by a flowery cloth, two sagging armchairs on either side of a fireplace, a longcase clock ticking in the corner. Astonishingly (because how could she have been expecting visitors in such an out-of-the-way place?) tea is already set out on the round table: slices of buttered bread, jars of strawberry jam and of honey, fruit cake, chocolate sponge, custard slices. The teapot is steaming, cups and saucers and plates laid out ready. It would be churlish to refuse such hospitality – and besides, there's nothing wrong in admitting to some hunger. It's been a while since those marmalade rolls on the beach.

So we sit with our host, who fills and refills our plate and cup generously, and chatters away so that we find ourselves immersed in a conversation about happy, small things – the weather, the tide, birds, music and the temperamental nature of long-case clocks. Small things, perhaps, but not inconsequential because this is the kind of conversation that creates a cushion of ease on which we can rest in the following silence.

'Those who've come a long way usually need a long rest,' she says suddenly. 'There's plenty of room here, if you like. No charge for friends!' Her laughter bubbles over until only the stoniest heart could hold back from joining in. 'Take your time!' She fills our cup again and nods at the next slice of chocolate sponge, then leaves the table to return to the piano. This time, the music is gentler, a kind of lullaby that rises, falls and rises to a comforting resolution, before beginning again, more quietly.

The Lord is my shepherd, I lack nothing.
He makes me lie down in green pastures, he leads me beside quiet
    waters, he refreshes my soul.
He guides me along the right paths for his name's sake.
Even though I walk through the darkest valley, I will fear no evil, for
    you are with me;
your rod and your staff, they comfort me.
You prepare a table before me in the presence of my enemies.
You anoint my head with oil; my cup overflows.

Surely your goodness and love will follow me all the days of my
    life,
and I will dwell in the house of the Lord for ever.
PSALM 23

We may have read this psalm many times, heard it in church services, perhaps shared it with others at moments of crisis. The Lord as loving shepherd is a staple image of religious art, and countless children have been tucked up for sleep beneath prints of the robed man (too often regrettably blond-haired) accompanied by a flock of clean white sheep. But the pastoral charm of such imagery is balanced by gritty resolve: this psalm is voiced by one who knows that they will pass through the 'darkest valley', who anticipates sitting down to break bread (a near-sacred symbol of welcome and hospitality in many cultures) in front of those who would do them harm. Anointing and blessing come unlooked-for, unearned – and the concluding lines speak of strong assurance that the Lord's grace and goodness are unending and unstoppable.

It is easy to overlook the fact that the guidance, refreshment and rest described in the opening verses are not in fact optional. The shepherd does not offer his flock the opportunity to sign up for a sabbatical, a take-it-or-leave-it bit of time out before the inevitable return to life at breakneck pace. We would do well to read the second sentence: 'He makes me lie down in green pastures, he leads me beside quiet waters…' Those who are part of the Lord's flock are made to stop, to draw breath, to sit down, to rest.

Sometimes, we need to be made to do this. Sometimes – for years, maybe – we end up so driven by our obligations (self-imposed or thrust upon us) that rest becomes, ridiculously, a suspect idea, a concession for the weak, for those lacking our iron resolve (iron that is rusting and crumbling beneath the stress of our brutal timetable). If our attention is forced to this fact, we may relent and allow ourselves to show a little mercy to ourselves. Not for too long, though, in case – in case what?

The question bears repetition: in case what? In case we lie on our deathbeds and wish we'd spent more time at the office? In case we fail to clinch one final deal after which life will at last break out into wine and roses? In case we disappoint our nearest and dearest whose resigned tolerance will flower into love if only we jump that final hurdle… or collapse trying?

We wake, we run full tilt at the day, and we may well carry on running until late into the night – and up and on into the next day, and the next, and the next, until that becomes the shape and pattern of decades, of a whole life. We forget how to slow down, let alone how to stop and catch our breath, rest (unless it's the tetchy, finger-drumming state of enforced idleness brought on by illness, endured for as short a time as necessary).

Rest is actually commanded in scripture, while work is taken for granted. There is no mandate for laziness, but observing a sabbath, hallowing it by rest after six days of labour, is non-negotiable for God's people. We are told more than once that even the Lord God rested after his work of creation (however long it took) – so who are we to deny ourselves a proper breather?

He makes us lie down. We can picture the shepherd leading his flock out of the sun's midday glare and into the shade of a great tree, where the grass is deeper and greener. There we, the sheep of his pasture, are obliged to rest under his watchful gaze, quite possibly for longer than we expect, until he notifies us that it is time to move on in search of the quiet waters, following the right paths that he will direct us to take, as and when we need to know.

Thus our wandering has brought us, unexpectedly, to a place of rest, a place of generous welcome and gratuitous hospitality. This is a place suffused with love at its most straightforward and undemanding. Such love is without strings attached, without hidden agendas or stressful demands. We are free to walk away, but this kind of unqualified warmth is alluring even to the most desiccated of souls. We feel a sudden, deep longing to be cared for – and the custard slices really are very good indeed.

The clock ticks; the music unfolds; more distantly, we can hear the waves lapping the shore of this island of green pastures.

We draw a deep breath.

We exhale a long sigh of something that feels, unsurprisingly, like relief.

We rest.

5

The blessing of sleep

We have come to the end of this strange, restful day. We have done a little talking and a lot of listening; we have wandered the low-lying slopes of the island. We have lain for a time in the shade of the few small trees; we have lunched and dined; we have been supplied before bedtime with hot chocolate and shortbread. We have climbed the creaky stairs to a small room, wallpapered with yellow roses and tucked beneath the eaves of the white stone cottage.

Cosy in a nest of blankets, we can just about hear the comforting noises of our host putting her home to bed – winding the clock, striking an unexpected but appropriate nocturne from the piano, closing the front door that has stood ajar throughout the day to let the breeze blow through.

'Good night!'

It may be a good night, for once, although for a while, with eyes closed, the bed feels as if it is rocking gently, as the kayak rocked on the sea for those many hours. Sleep comes, in the end, as the softest of waves.

It couldn't last, though.

The subconscious teasingly plays a flickering reel of memory – and plays it to a false ending. In a dream of calm night-time gliding, the kayak suddenly flips for no reason, spilling us head first into heart-stoppingly cold, perhaps fathomless water. Waking with a frantic gasp for air, we open our eyes and see darkness so dense as to disorientate completely. Reaching out wildly, our fingers identify nothing. Eyes strain and dilate, hallucinating a windowless prison cell instead of the small bedroom.

Fear tightens like an metal band round the chest. We gasp again, stretch out terrified hands to stop the walls closing in – and brush curtains that, dragged aside, uncover a merciful rectangle of fainter black. Fumbling, shaking, we find a handle and wrench it open. Cool air floods in, and slowly the waking world returns. The rectangle of fainter black resolves itself into familiar patterns of stars. Heart thuds hard, skipping a beat or two, and then resumes its usual rhythm. All is well, as it has been here since our arrival, in fact. Sleep is unlikely to return for a while, though, and that is a bitter thought because the bed was so warm and the coverings so cosy – and oblivion had been so welcome.

Here's a thought: slip on enough clothes to keep out the early hours' chill, tiptoe out of the bedroom, down the stairs (keeping to the edge to minimise creaking), and hope to remember the way to the front door, anticipating that our host has not bothered to use locks or bolts. The door to what must be her bedroom is not closed – she, at least, is enjoying uninterrupted rest, snoring lightly.

We're feeling wide awake now and vision has adjusted to starlight levels of illumination. It's all the more astonishing, then, when we step outside and see a huge ball of moon starting to climb above the horizon, almost as bright as day. The sense of invitation to walk out into the silver light is irresistible. The green hills are tinted grey now and the shoreline is a jumble of bleached shadows – but the kayak is still safely pulled up where we left it earlier. The thought of eventually having to move on from this place is uninviting, to say the least.

We climb the slope above the house, treading carefully in the tricky light, pause for breath – and catch it, in shock and then delight, as a bird begins to sing in the thicket ahead. A nightingale? Here? Unlikely… but, hey, no more unlikely than coming across a jolly white-haired woman with a longcase clock and a honky-tonk piano on an island located who knows where. The birdsong ebbs and flows, louder and softer again and piercingly sweet, as the moon continues its slow arc across the sky and we stand still, captivated in this dazzling darkness.

When the song has finally finished, the memories of panicked waking from fear-filled dreams have dissipated. It takes a while to recognise the feeling that has flowed like warm oil through our being.

The feeling is peacefulness – and a measure of peace that we have not experienced for more years than we can remember.

We need not scrutinise it, anxiously, for appropriate characteristics and durability. We need not worry whether to categorise it as 'peace through the end of conflict' or 'peace in the eye of the storm' or even 'peace because a task is complete'. We need not do so, because even as we find our shoulders dropping, our muscles releasing tension so fast that we almost drop to our knees, we sense an inner voice reminding us to take this proffered gift and enjoy rather than examine it.

'Because,' whispers the voice, 'you will need this memory to sustain you on the way ahead.'

Does there have to be a way ahead? Put aside that thought and its associated baggage, which is no sooner articulated than it starts insinuating itself into the consciousness like an icy draught. Stand still in the dazzling darkness; breathe deep; listen as the nightingale song is renewed and the sea sighs and sighs again over the little beach; feel the flow of peace, a holy oil bringing blessing as it touches every fibre of heart and mind and body. Hold the feeling, hold the cool, fresh air, hold the song and the night sounds. Remember how this darkness is not dark at all but a different kind of light. Then, at last, begin to walk back to where the whitewashed cottage waits for us, door still open for us, staircase leading round a turn and up to the room under the eaves, where we can curl up once again in the warm nest of blankets, finding that the peace is still within us, still flowing and blessing.

And then we sleep… and sleep… and sleep.

I lift up my eyes to the mountains – where does my help come from?
My help comes from the Lord, the Maker of heaven and earth.
He will not let your foot slip – he who watches over you will not slumber;
indeed, he who watches over Israel will neither slumber nor sleep.
The Lord watches over you – the Lord is your shade at your right hand;
the sun will not harm you by day, nor the moon by night.
The Lord will keep you from all harm – he will watch over your life;
the Lord will watch over your coming and going both now and for evermore.
PSALM 121

Sleep is a blessing, but one that we so easily spurn or at least treat too casually. Generations of children have been sent to bed as a punishment; generations of teenagers fight against parental curfews intended to ensure enough rest; generations of adults squeeze every last minute of waking time out of the 24-hour span and, as long as we delude ourselves that our planet's power supplies are inexhaustible, we will continue to burn the literal and metaphorical oil way past midnight.

When troubles and stresses crowd in upon us, however, sleep can become an elusive treasure, the harder to find the more we seek it.

Losing the ability to sleep, to rest mind and body, could be defined as a form of torture. Instead of space for release of said troubles and stresses, we find ourselves on a mental rack, wound tighter and tighter without mercy. We may wake in the smallest hours, trembling as if we were locked away in a dark box, struggling to escape our terrible fears, which grow fiercer and more monstrous as we lie there, fearing them. Even when morning comes, we find only momentary relief because we know that night will come again – and we have lost the blessing of sleep.

The gentle repetition of our psalm soothes like a lullaby: 'he watches over you… he watches over you… the Lord watches over you'. Not only now but in the days and nights to come, 'the Lord watches over you' – and so we can rest, and not only rest but fall asleep. The Lord is vigilant on our behalf, so we need not struggle to stay awake, keeping watchful eyes on our worries in case they give us the slip and start to work their mischief. Whether by day or by night, whether we need shade from the desert sun or guidance for a moonlit journey, the Lord is there, watchful, guarding, protecting.

That does not mean, of course, that we live in shatterproof glass bubbles, cocooned from any kind of harm. What it does mean is that even in the worst of times, we can still turn to the one whose presence dwarfs the highest mountains, whose loving gaze outshines all terrestrial and celestial lights, the working out of whose purposes extends from before the beginning into a future which unfolds eternally.

Watching someone we love as they sleep is a particular intimacy, as we see them at their most defenceless. Indeed, sleep seems so close to death that we often fear for our newborn babies in their sleep, hovering over them to check that they are still breathing. Cuddling a sick or frightened child in the night is costly, committed parenting, which can be experienced not only as love but also as healing. And to sit beside someone who cannot sleep is to offer tender, comforting presence, even if no physical touch is exchanged.

Thus, says the psalmist, will the Lord watch over us as we sleep. When we wake, sweat-soaked after bad dreams, when we grope the bedside table blindly to reassure ourselves that the real world is still there, when we lie awake afraid of never finding a way through the maze of dilemmas and hard decisions – the Lord is watching over us, now and for evermore.

It is probably just before dawn that another dream comes. This time, we experience not a nightmare plunge into an oceanic abyss but something that teases the mind on waking, starting to slip away even as we try to recall it for further examination.

In the dream we stand barefoot on a cracked tile floor, awash with warmish water that has sluiced slimy detritus into the corners – a used sticking plaster, squashed paper tissues, a twine of long black hair. Ahead, we see a row of door-less, paperless toilets, to the right a line of shower cubicles with torn plastic curtains. To the left a tap drips loudly into a huge sink and, further off, a cistern gurgles as it tries and fails to fill, on and on.

In the dream we approach the sink, noting the grime on every angle of its fussy china moulding. And the soap – the soap is layered with filth that does not bear analysis. We turn our eyes from the damp hand towel hanging underneath. Anyone who tried to wash here would leave dirtier than they arrived, yet (as is the way in dreams) we know that we came here in the hope of getting clean.

Then (as is the way in dreams) the scene fades abruptly into waking. Stretching in our nest of blankets, we hear the encouraging sound of a kettle boiling and we smell toast. Our host is singing (loudly but tunefully) as she moves about the kitchen, and the glow through the curtains suggests that the new day has begun with sunshine.

The dream memory lingers, though, a stale exhalation from a hidden cupboard of the heart that has swung open by itself. It lingers even in the steam of the spotless bathroom that opens off the kitchen. It lingers as we seat ourselves at the breakfast table. It lingers to remind us that, whether we like it or not, whether we understand it or not, our journey has only just begun.

6

No place like home

This place, this white stone cottage, could suit us very well, on reflection. The thing is, generous hospitality is rather seductive, once accepted. A warm bed, clean bathroom, plentiful food and abundant cups of tea make for comfort bordering on luxury. True, our heart of hearts tells us that we are being babied, a little, and that undemanding, apparently endless giving is probably not the best context for growing up and moving on (but why might we want to bother with trying that, having messed up so badly before?)... but the hours pass happily. There is morning and there is evening and there is morning and there is evening and there is morning again, and gratitude starts to become expectation, teetering on the brink of assumption.

She is no fool, though, this host of ours. On the third morning, she passes the toast, she smiles as broadly as before, and then she gently but uncompromisingly lets us know that this time of rest and respite is coming to an end.

'No charge for friends,' she tells us, as she first told us what seems like weeks ago now. 'I'm always happy to pop the kettle on the stove and open the cake tin – so long as you take me as you find me.' Her eyes are clearest blue and they survey us with disconcerting clarity. 'But don't forget that this is a shelter for you just for now. It's a resting-place on your journey. It's not the finishing post.'

The tea sits undrunk; the last slice of toast cools to a leathery mat; a cloud has passed over the sun; the wind through the open door is cold. Of course we have no permanent place here. Of course this is not home – and of course there is that unsettling dream that demands some sort of response (and, truth be told, at some point during each night since arrival, we have found ourselves back in that dirty public bathroom, flinching from every surface). But the sea currents brought us here and, on reflection, we could do much worse than settle here by way of an ending. Even playing at settling down is much pleasanter than facing uncertainty – and as we feel the return to uncertainty, we begin to feel anxious, and that leads to anger.

Stupid, honky-tonk woman! How can she possibly imagine what it is like to be us with the agonies we have survived, the disappointments and upsets we have endured. We haven't begun to tell her the story of how life has let us down, how we never got the breaks we deserved (not being in the right place at the right time and not born with the right sort of silver spoon and so on), and how badly we have been treated by those who should have known better, and how – basically – none of this is our fault. In fact, taking into account our litany of hardships and disappointments, we have done rather well to be sitting here at the breakfast table at all.

The next thought – of leaving this table and this place where peace beyond comprehension has trickled into our heart – slices through the anger to expose our desolation underneath. To end up homeless and rootless through our own bad choices was miserable enough. To be, in effect, asked to move on from somewhere that has begun to give us a smidgeon of stability is surely cruel and unusual punishment. Self-pity crumples the face, bringing tears that flow more freely as the sense of injustice grows and awareness of loss intensifies.

Our host does not rush in with comfort nor does she rescind her gentle, uncompromising words. Calmly, she clears the breakfast cups and plates. Calmly, she sits down at the piano and starts to play and carries on playing until the jazzy chords snag our attention sufficiently to check the weeping. In effect, we have made an emotional scene to try and get our own way. Rightly, it has had no effect on this stately matriarch, whose plump hands shift seamlessly from melody to melody.

'Finding home is a gift,' she says without turning her head, so we have to lean in to catch her words. 'Once you've discovered that homecoming feeling, you don't forget it but, dear me, it's easy to take it for granted, silly folk that we are. Sleep – now there's another gift.' And this time she shoots a bright blue glance over her shoulder. 'Sleep and rest and peace and home – they should be the air we breathe as children so that we remember, growing up, how life is supposed to feel.

'And if you never get the chance to breathe that air – or you've breathed so much bad stuff that you've forgotten what the good stuff should smell like – well, you risk waking up one day and finding you've locked yourself in an airless room and gone and lost the key. You've no idea how to get out and things start to get a bit desperate, don't they? But if you break the door down to escape, that's a lot of mess to be clearing up, isn't it? Perhaps you're so desperate, though, you feel there's no alternative.

'And if you get out of that room, what then? Do you go looking for somewhere or someone that reminds you of the good, clean air of home and sleep and rest and peace, all of it, all at once? That's a big ask, isn't it? A bit like chasing the wind... And then' – she stops playing and turns right round to look at us, smiling with great kindness – 'then you can end up in a right old pickle.'

Somehow, instead of more angry, self-pitying tears, her words and kindness and broadening smile evoke a small smile in return, a smile that turns to a small laugh that grows to what could almost be described as a chuckle. Now she is laughing with us at our predicament because, to be honest, the whole situation has its ridiculous side. And in that laughter, there is blessing.

How lovely is your dwelling-place, Lord Almighty!
My soul yearns, even faints, for the courts of the Lord;
my heart and my flesh cry out for the living God.
Even the sparrow has found a home, and the swallow a nest for
*   herself,*
where she may have her young – a place near your altar,
Lord Almighty, my King and my God.
Blessed are those who dwell in your house; they are ever praising
*   you.*
Blessed are those whose strength is in you, whose hearts are set on
*   pilgrimage.*
As they pass through the Valley of Baka, they make it a place of
*   springs;*
the autumn rains also cover it with pools.
They go from strength to strength, till each appears before God in
*   Zion…*
Better is one day in your courts than a thousand elsewhere;
I would rather be a doorkeeper in the house of my God
than dwell in the tents of the wicked.
For the Lord God is a sun and a shield; the Lord bestows favour and
*   honour;*
no good thing does he withhold from those whose way of life is
*   blameless.*

PSALM 84:1–7, 10–11

Finding a space to settle, somewhere to rest and nurture and be nurtured, is a fundamental instinct of living creatures. Even birds and insects who migrate enormous distances will find their way back to the same stopping-off points along the way and reappear to spend summer or winter in the same places. The dislocation caused by loss of home is profound, evidenced by the long process of adjustment experienced even by those who have found new homes after escaping persecution or conflict. Finding a new place to live may be a matter of survival – and a cause for huge relief and thanks – but the process of making that place 'home' may nevertheless prove arduous. When we are torn up by our roots, we should not expect to bloom again immediately after being replanted.

Like our mother tongue, that first language in which we learned to express our thoughts and understand ourselves, memories of our childhood home (or the earliest one we recall) are an influence so fundamental that it can pervade, unnoticed, the rest of our lives. What is it about that architectural style or shade of curtains, or wallpaper, or garden shrub? Oh yes – we had one like that when we were growing up and, ever since, it has provided an unconscious template, an archetype, for what constitutes home.

Accordingly, it is the more problematic when that 'home' template is associated with neither security nor love, but with some level of loss or trauma. Never having experienced security, we do not know how or where to find it. But that does not stop us searching – and in doing so (in the words of the not-so-stupid honky-tonk woman) we can end up in a right old pickle.

The people of God know where home lies: in the dwelling-place of the Lord Almighty. In the days of the psalmist, that would have meant the temple in Jerusalem, and the vivid word-pictures of this particular psalm evoke the birds flying in and out of the precincts, energetically nest-building despite the busy surroundings. They have found safety in God's house and so are envied by the one who longs even for the lowly job of doorkeeper, just to have a toehold in that place of total belonging.

The shining protection of the Lord offers more than shelter, however. Those who are blessed and strengthened by it are also summoned to pilgrimage. Part of that pilgrimage is about having work to do – detailed by the psalmist as environmental improvements, working in tandem with prevailing climatic conditions – which results in a dry wasteland flowing with water, imagery with obvious spiritual implications. We are strengthened in order to go out and serve; pilgrimage means resolute journeying that finally brings us to our true home, which is in the presence of our Father God.

'I don't have a map for the journey you're making,' she says, setting out on the table a row of waterproof containers for biscuits, dried fruit, cheese, chocolate, hard-boiled eggs and beef jerky, and three large bottles of water. 'But this might come in handy.' It's a compass, almost small enough to have popped out of a Christmas cracker. 'And don't worry, you haven't drifted as far as you might have thought. Keep your nerve, paddle a steady course, and you'll come through all right.'

We have told her the story of the men who found their way to the island of hidden valleys and waterfalls and she nodded in unsurprised approval, although we had not yet expressed (even to ourselves) the intention of making that our destination.

'And,' she continues, as together we carry the supplies down to the waiting kayak, along with a waterproof cape ('just in case it rains'), 'when you're ready to head back to where you came from, just point your nose east, where the sun rises. It'll take you a bit of pulling but you'll be strong enough by then.'

Head back? Where bridges of every kind have been burned after we crossed them? Where nothing and nobody ever wants to cross our path again?

Fat chance.

'What did I say, friend?' She interrupts our moody thoughts. 'I said, "When you're ready." And that means later; it doesn't mean now, not yet it doesn't. One day, you'll try a door that you thought was bolted with ten bolts to keep you out for ever and ever – and it will open for you. Look over there' – she nods in a north-westerly direction. 'That's where you want to be heading for next, I think.'

We see a shadowy line, suggesting hilly contours against what is, for now, a sunlit sky. It appears to be a manageable trip (although, again, don't try this at home, kids) but testing enough to induce a pleasing shiver of excitement. We have moved on from aimless, hopeless wandering; now, we feel the first whispers of a summons to (whisper it) pilgrimage.

Part 3

Ruins

7

Into the depths

It's hard to know exactly how much time has passed – exact reckoning of minutes and hours feels less relevant than noting the progression of the sun across the sky and the steady pace at which the low green hills of the island of respite have faded from view. It's hard to know, too, whether distance has started to draw a veil across the hilly contours ahead – or whether a curtain of rain has descended. No weather forecast was offered before our departure, despite the general advice and helpful provisions, but surely we are safe in assuming that we would have heard at least a few words of warning if conditions looked set to turn nasty. Anyway, our next port of call looks promisingly closer than at the outset of our trip; we are definitely making progress; we have purpose; we will have ventured and we will have gained… and we permit ourselves a little pre-emptive self-congratulation. And why not, after everything we have come through? Well done, us.

If only the wind was at our back and not in our face.

If only the waters were a bit less choppy.

If only we could push down permanently the flutter of unease in the pit of the stomach.

If only we could switch off completely the nagging voice in the inner ear: 'It's further than you think… you're not as strong as you reckon… and night will fall before you're ready for it.'

Paddle. Rest and drift a little way. Paddle. Rest and drift more slowly because the wind is picking up. Paddle. Rest for a few breaths and then start paddling again, as we feel ourselves inexorably veering off course, as wind and currents collude to set us on a sideways trajectory. How very puny and frail we are, balanced in a tiny chip of fibreglass and caught between grey water and grey cloud. And now the sky is darkening in the west – and now the wind is starting to snatch at the paddle and now the prow is slopping up and down through mounting waves that could grow until they swamp us altogether.

Steady now. Don't forget to breathe. Keep on keeping on. Keep calm and eat two squares of chocolate. If all else fails, something will turn up… probably.

And then it's too late.

There's no time left to formulate Plan B (or C or D) or check that there is enough strength in reserve. The storm starts to break upon us.

Before long it is as if every point of the compass has disappeared, as if sea and sky have vanished, leaving us spinning on a deadly rollercoaster, blasted by water cannons that fire without mercy, without warning, from every direction. Somehow or other, we stay upright even as the white horses trample us. Somehow or other, the paddle is frozen in our grip although we cannot hope to use it to steer. Every scrap of strength clenches around the will to hold on… and on… and on, between one snatched lungful of air and the next. In a remote backroom of the brain, recalibration of possibilities continues: at least we have supplies. At least we're afloat. At least we still have a paddle. This won't last for ever. We have come so far, survived so much – this can't be the end, not now we've managed to find some small sense of purpose. Please.

We look up, wiping the salt from our bleared eyes – and here really is the end approaching fast. Here is a rogue wave, a monster wall of water climbing lazily higher and higher, opening a gulf before us into which we are poured, helpless passengers on this ride from hell.

Wipe-out.

We feel ourselves rush down, down, down to the deepest depths, final thoughts floating above our head like our last bubbles of oxygen as we are mashed in the maelstrom. Everything is thunder and turmoil and choking and blackness – and then, beyond belief, our head breaks the surface and air, not water, fills our lungs. And there, banging against us in the boiling surf, is the kayak – or rather, what's left of it. Jagged fibreglass shreds the fingers but we clutch hard for life's sake, willing shaky limbs to kick with the suck and surge of the currents in the hope of being carried eventually towards solid ground, even if it's no more than a ridge of rock.

The air is still thick with storm spray, but we can make out the bulk of what is surely land, looming to our right. The rain has stopped, the wind is easing at last, but the sea remains mountainous. The effort of survival leaves no space for fear; if we make it to tomorrow, we can revisit these hours and have the luxury of shuddering. For now, we endure – just about, but as the cold seeps to our core, strength begins to drain away. The sea continues to boil, the white horses running angrily ahead of the fading wind, and we float, empty as a seed husk, towards the shadowy coast.

Everything is growing darker.

A movement catches at the edge of vision, something shooting past us through the heaving water. There – gone – and now there – and gone before we can focus on what we have seen. Surely that was not a face? Yet there it is again, enormous eyes gazing into ours for a long moment before the sleek whiskered head slips down and away, reappearing ahead to check out the human interloper from another angle. Now there are two of them, a pair of seals circling us watchfully, almost thoughtfully.

We are not completely alone in this watery wilderness – and simply shaping that idea has the side effect of rebooting thought. We are not alone and, by raising the head, it is possible to see how close we have now come to land, although nothing is visible except dauntingly steep cliffs. The sea swell threatens to smash us against them, but a final, feeble spurt of kicking brings us round what proves to be a headland, as the seals swim almost at our shoulder, as if urging us onwards. Beyond the headland, in the very last of the light, a shingle beach opens up before us.

Save me, O God, for the waters have come up to my neck.
I sink in the miry depths, where there is no foothold.
I have come into the deep waters; the floods engulf me.
I am worn out calling for help; my throat is parched.
My eyes fail, looking for my God.
Those who hate me without reason outnumber the hairs of my
    head;
many are my enemies without cause, those who seek to destroy
    me.
I am forced to restore what I did not steal.
You, God, know my folly; my guilt is not hidden from you…
Do not let the floodwaters engulf me or the depths swallow me up
or the pit close its mouth over me.
Answer me, Lord, out of the goodness of your love; in your great
    mercy turn to me…
The Lord hears the needy and does not despise his captive people.
Let heaven and earth praise him, the seas and all that move in
    them,
for God will save Zion and rebuild the cities of Judah.
PSALM 69:1–5, 15–16, 33–35

The Psalms remind us constantly how bad things happen to those who do not count themselves as particularly bad people. We hear in these verses from one who acknowledges their 'folly', indeed 'guilt', but who still cries out for rescue from a situation of overwhelming disaster, which is not (or not wholly) of their own making. Yes, they made mistakes, but now they find themselves forced to offer recompense far beyond what is reasonable; they are being punished for wrongdoings of which they are innocent. As the psalm as a whole makes clear, the speaker is finding accusation and attack wherever they turn. They face estrangement from those they love; they face public mockery and humiliation. The metaphorical mud being flung at them is not just sticking but turning out to be part of a swamp that will suck them down altogether, unless God hears their cry for help.

We do not know and so cannot unravel the whys and wherefores of the original situation – who was in the right, who was indisputably in the wrong. What is unequivocal is the stark honesty with which the speaker in the psalm addresses their predicament. They concede that they are not faultless, yet they cry out passionately against the disproportionate suffering inflicted upon them. 'This was not deserved and so, God, you need to do something,' they shout at the heavens. 'Be who you are, be the Lord Almighty, and save me, because nobody else can.'

The overall witness of scripture to the nature of the God we worship is equally unequivocal: this is the creator of 'heaven and earth... the seas and all that move in them', one who is in covenant relationship with his children, and we can trust that this God will hear us and rescue us. Even if we can do no more than cling to a life raft of divine promises, of stories of the Lord's deliverance remembered from our own lives or the lives of others – that will prove, in the end, to be enough. 'I know,' cries the psalmist, 'that the Lord hears the needy. I know that he cares for the captives. In fact, I feel such a surge of hope that it lifts me to my feet in praise. I declare to any and all who will listen that God is in the business of rebuilding, of setting things right again. I declare to any and all who will listen that God is good, all the time.'

We can easily forget the old stories of God's saving power, especially if we are drowning in a storm, simply hanging on not so much in hope of rescue as because we are stubbornly refusing to let go. We may have strayed so far, for so long, that when that saving power draws near us, we do not recognise it. Mercifully, however, such salvation is impossible to earn; we can never deserve it. It comes to us as the gift of love; what we must do is choose whether or not to receive it.

As the waves crash on the shore, the noise echoes thunderously against the cliffs lining the beach and blocking out most of the sky. We are floating towards a rusting metal jetty presumably once intended for loading and unloading goods from the roofless shed that lies above the tideline. Scrabbling for purchase on the sea floor, we finally touch something solid – but it feels like more corroded metal, submerged and caked in long weeds that reach out to snag us. There is just enough time to kick away and thrash against the undertow that would keep us spinning helplessly just beyond the safety of the shallows.

The seals have gone, unless they are still bobbing up and down in deeper water, watching to see what we do next. It is too dark to tell. We struggle forward and forward again as the waves pummel us – it's the last gasp – and we flounder, stagger, and finally collapse, freezing water still breaking over us as we sprawl on solid ground. We have reached land, but along the way we have lost almost everything. Even the last scrap of splintered kayak is floating away behind us.

As we limp higher up, no plan in mind except to find anything that will offer a bit of shelter until morning comes, the shingle grinds far too loudly. In the heavy twilight, the gaping doorway of the ruined shed looks watchful – and for an unpleasant moment, we imagine something moving there, something shifting quickly out of sight.

Maybe we did... maybe we did not... but the darkness exudes a feeling that is not benign, not one of welcome.

We have been spared, again, although we cannot articulate by what or whom this has come about. Our souls cried out in the depths and we find ourselves returned to relative safety – but with increasing emphasis on 'relative', it would seem.

Stand still – and hear how beneath the crash of the waves, there is silence, perhaps (push that thought away quickly) a listening silence. There cannot be anything listening (can there?) because this feels like a deserted – a desert – place. And it is so very, very cold.

8

A desert place

Eyes snap open, senses on full alert. What has woken us?

Nothing stirs; even the grey light seems fixed, frozen. It must be morning but the air is, if anything, colder than before. Limbs so stiff as to restrict movement to a crawl, we venture out from the approximate shelter of the roofless shed where we spent the night hours crouching and sometimes dozing. There's no point in staying here with no food, no water, no means of warmth – but the chance of finding another kindly host in this desert place looks beyond unlikely. It feels like the final stroke of bad fortune to find that our mobile phone is dead. Thoughtfully sealed in a plastic bag by our previous host, it has ended up immersed in seawater that has somehow seeped in. Anyway, what chance of a signal here? This place takes the idea of 'alone' to a whole new level.

A twisting path cuts across the intersection between shore and cliff face, leading in the direction of a series of lumpy hills. The going is rough, the ground a mess of bramble-covered detritus left over from whatever industrial works once took place here. Walking brings a bit of warmth back to the body and relief is a spur too, relief at leaving behind the oppressive cliff-hung beach. But the light is not growing, despite the passing minutes, and, if anything, the silence hangs heavier than before, throbbing in the ears.

Topping a rise brings us on to a plateau rammed tight against the lumpy hills that crowd towards the sea. There, at the end of the twisting path, stands a huge house, not in ruins but showing no signs of life either. What realistic choice do we have but to see what lies within? Even so, our prickling unease is turning to fear that causes breath to catch in the throat, eyes stretched wide in anticipation of threat from every possible angle.

We approach the house and its rows of staring windows through a square of what was once a garden but is now a tangle of dead shrubs blanketed in bindweed. Overgrown heaps of prunings and the ashy traces of a bonfire hint at long-ago attempts at clearance. The front door does not offer handle or knocker, but a push at the flaking paintwork opens it sufficiently to allow entry. Right now, though, we are far from sure that entry is what we want.

Hesitating in the doorway, listening for we don't know what, trying not to keep looking behind us – that is not what we want either. Cold and hunger (not curiosity and certainly not courage) eventually drive us to step into a long hall, moving soundlessly to avoid disturbing whatever might be waiting here. The parquet flooring is gritty underfoot as we pass a succession of closed doors and on to what must have once been a kitchen. Now it is just a room heaped with broken cupboards, piled up as if ready for a renovation that never happened. There's no sign of anything to eat and no water in the pipes jutting from the wall.

So it's back to the hall and the closed doors, every one of which refuses to open. The feeling of being watched – or listened to – is slowly intensifying, but we still cannot see any tangible signs that someone (or something) has disturbed this place for years, even decades. A staircase leads straight up to a corridor where a long-desiccated weeping fig stands by an empty bookcase. At least here the doors are unlocked, but they lead to rooms so crammed with musty furniture that further exploration is pretty much impossible. Round a corner – and here we find the passage dividing, left and right. Taking the left-hand way leads us to the top of a set of narrow stairs that plunge into shadows, perhaps descending to the used-to-be kitchen, perhaps to somewhere even mustier and darker.

Then – unmistakeably – we hear stealthy movement down below, in the musty dark. Someone – or something – is at the foot of those stairs. Someone – or something – has paused, perhaps listening for our listening.

Time to run.

Whatever may or may not be coming behind us, we don't wait to discover. Whatever we may or may not disturb in our crashing flight, we don't care. But somehow or other we mistake the way back to the main stairs and, round another corner (that we don't recall from earlier), we find that the only way ahead takes us up yet again, up clattering wooden treads to a small landing, a door on either side, a mossy skylight overhead.

Which door?

Go right. It opens.

The room beyond is bigger than we expected, although as with every other room, it is jammed and crammed with furniture. We see mismatched armchairs and settees pushed randomly together, and a shadeless standard lamp. A trelliswork screen partitions off the rear end – and behind the screen, we sense, rather than see, a presence.

In the poised instant before we turn tail and flee, a throat is cleared.

A hoarse voice speaks: 'Don't – don't be afraid.'

The words drop like stones in the heavy air.

Then the voice speaks again: 'I've been here for so long... so alone.' And the presence moves and becomes a person, stepping out from behind the screen until we are face to face. 'Please... Please, let me talk to you.'

At first glance, they are very old; at second glance, a better word might be 'seasoned'. Wrinkles suggest longevity, but the direct gaze suggests command of thought and purpose. They are not stooped, but they move slowly, approaching as we take a nervous pace or two back. What do they want? Why are they here? Who on earth are they?

Stretching out a wrinkled hand, they indicate a pair of faded red velvet chairs, angled towards one another.

'Sit with me… please?' A sideways glance. 'Or – do you have another engagement?'

This ghost of a joke (if joke it is) is so unexpected – and our nerves strung so tight – that it is hard to stifle a laugh. What have we to lose? What else have we to do?

Nothing.

We sit – and then we find that we are listening to the hoarse voice telling a story, their story, begun without preliminary chit-chat, without our permission sought. And it's an unexpectedly familiar story of careless choices, wilful choices, commitments abandoned, duties neglected. We hear of catastrophes unfolding, the sky falling in and eventual retreat to this room at the top of this broken house in this desert place. They speak of a daily reality that is simply endurance; they describe a world that has shrivelled to an outlook so bleak that it appears to have no hope of ending.

My days vanish like smoke; my bones burn like glowing embers.
My heart is blighted and withered like grass; I forget to eat my
*   food.*
In my distress I groan aloud and am reduced to skin and bones.
I am like a desert owl, like an owl among the ruins.

I lie awake; I have become like a bird alone on a roof.
All day long my enemies taunt me; those who rail against me use
my name as a curse.
For I eat ashes as my food and mingle my drink with tears because
of your great wrath,
for you have taken me up and thrown me aside.
My days are like the evening shadow; I wither away like grass.
But you, Lord, sit enthroned for ever; your renown endures through
all generations...
Let this be written for a future generation,
that a people not yet created may praise the Lord:
'The Lord looked down from his sanctuary on high, from heaven he
viewed the earth,
to hear the groans of the prisoners and release those condemned
to death.'

PSALM 102:3–12, 18–20

When we come into a time of crisis or even catastrophe, the final humiliation can be admitting quite how low we have been brought. For as long as we possibly can, we deny what is happening to us and, especially, how our situation may appear to others. We may present ourselves to ourselves (and to any and all who will listen) as martyrs for an unimpeachable cause, victims who have been forced, quite against their will, into this or that stratagem that led, quite unforeseen, to our present mess.

As is often the case in the Psalms, the speaker here blames 'enemies' for the situation they find themselves in, as well as the 'great wrath' of the Lord. The tone may sound almost petulant – but the baseline is, as before, unflinching honesty. We cannot hope to be rescued if we are not clear about needing rescue and if we are afraid to ask for it. The danger is that we are disabled from allowing ourselves to break down and admit our hopeless state, by the many coping strategies that have been drilled into us by the time we reach adulthood. How much better, how much more grown-up it feels to use the terminology of 'coping' and 'getting by' instead of doing as the psalmist does here and more or less howling with despair: 'Look at me – look at me! Look at what I've been reduced to! As you have brought me to this, O Lord, so I call on you to sort it out. Now.'

Of course we can never set terms and conditions on what the Lord will or will not do for us – or when or where or how the Lord might act. It may be, though, that we do ourselves no favours when we expect a divine airlift out of disaster, the extent of which only becomes apparent as we are lifted safely above it. Maybe the process is more interactive than that. Maybe rescue can become a way not of reducing us to passivity but of helping us to discover our God-given strength. Maybe it is the impetus we need to force us to seek maturity. We are called to be trusting, like children; we are also called to grow up, spiritually speaking.

When we come to the point of acknowledging our despondency, our brokenness, our ruin, we can acknowledge, too, that we have one on whom we can call, one who, in the words of the psalmist, sits 'enthroned for ever'. Bewailing human futility does not mean forgetting that the Lord's eternal reign encompasses all that was, all that is and all that will be. And while the poetry speaks of God looking down from heaven, the coming of his Son demands that we balance such transcendence with immanence, *El Shaddai* with Emmanuel. Our Father is God Almighty but also God with us.

As we listen to the tale told in this airless, cluttered attic room, we do not get answers to every one of the questions we would like to ask. We don't get to clarify the exact whys and wherefores, but we see, beyond denial, that we are face to face with someone who is in some way a portent to us. The tale they tell us could be heard as a warning that we would be ill-advised to ignore, given the journey that has brought us here. Chance after chance after chance comes and goes – chances to confess, to own up (to ourselves as well as to others) to what is really going on, chances to step into the light. And if every chance is missed or ignored, then eventually we face what feels like the last reckoning. Then, the dregs of 'could be' become 'didn't'; 'might be' becomes 'wouldn't'. Everything that matters becomes past tense; we become a remnant of our own life, with nothing to do in the slow hours left to us except mull over our regrets.

And now the hoarse voice has finished. We see now that there are tears falling silently down the wrinkled cheeks – yet we cannot think of anything to offer by way of comfort, cold, hungry, thirsty and exhausted as we are. The temptation is so strong to exit, to back out of the cramped space, hurrying downstairs on legs that are still strong enough for escape, heading out into the bleak daytime and seeing what turns up (as something so often has). The temptation is so strong to forget the reality of the journey we ourselves have made, to overlook the rain-soaked wandering, the huddling in the cave, the hopeless drifting over the sea – even the horrors of the storm. Unlike this old, broken stranger we don't give up the game so quickly, do we? We're still a player, aren't we? We can summon up strength for one more throw of the dice, one more toss of the coin, trying for one more kiss from Lady Luck.

Then the one who has shared their story so openly reaches out and takes our hand. The direct gaze will not let us look away. 'Thank you for listening. I feel better now.'

A pause – and they speak the two words that refuse denial of the bond that (whether we like it or not) they have made between us: 'Help me.'

9

A time to mend

How could we – derelict, washed up as we are – help anyone? The only thing we can do is listen, but that seems (at this point, anyway) to be enough. As we continue to listen to the reflections that follow the story, the weighing of dilemmas thrown up by what has happened in the past, we are reminded that sometimes reality can be unbearable. We are shown that sometimes the only viable option for a time is to hide away from the agonising details of our mistakes. That may not bring much peace or joy – but sometimes, closing eyes and ears to what others are pointing out means the difference between coping and sinking. And, for whatever reason, someone may not be able to contemplate the slightest risk of sinking, at least for now. They see (even as others try to correct their seeing) that too much and too many depend on their coping. Call them deluded, call them perverse, call them stupid – but do them the courtesy of respecting their decision to limp on, blind and deaf, for as long as they can. And they may well not want your pity either.

That is part of what we have learned from the story told by the attic-room stranger. Their life led them on just such a path for a time. We have also learned this: that the ruined places through which someone is stumbling can bring them, finally, to their knees. They are too badly injured to continue alone – and so they need another to help them up again, gently, and ask them what they want. They simply need another to walk with them through the ruined places – and to hold back from trying to fix them because tidiness is more congenial than mess. Above all, they can't be hurried. Walking with them will probably take more time than (at least at first) we are comfortable giving.

The story that we have heard has traced a trajectory from limping along, eyes and ears closed to everything except the imperative to keep going, to reaching the point of collapse. We have sat and listened, even though we have been almost incoherent with fatigue, repeatedly spooked by shadows and furtive noises echoing from time to time up the stairwell. Sometimes we have been on the verge of running straight out of the door again – as we have run away from similar situations so many times before.

But we haven't run away, not this time. We have moved to a more comfortable seat on a sagging sofa; we have begun to feel an unlikely connection with this person who has been solitary for so long. And this unlikely connection has – without our noticing – begun to loosen the stranglehold of what we realise is our own self-absorption. We have found ourselves able to focus with compassion on the state of heart and mind of another human being.

The day has been passing and the light changing, and now the window set in the ceiling shows a square of bright evening sky. Nauseous through lack of food, we have eaten a proffered slice of rather dry bread; we have drunk the black tea prepared for us – and we have been thankful.

'Thank you.' The voice is less hoarse now, vocal cords limbered up after what has felt like weeks of talking. 'And, you know, I think it's time for me to let the work begin. They've been waiting so long for me to give the word but I wasn't ready. But, you know, I am ready now… and that's because you listened… to the very end. And that helped me. So… come with me.'

Together we rise from the sagging sofa. Together we walk slowly through the door and leave that airless attic room. One after the other (the stairs are treacherous in the half-light), we descend right down to the hallway. They are leading us towards the shattered kitchen which, surely, is also the way to the foot of the backstairs where someone or something had been listening and waiting.

Don't go that way, please.

But what is this?

Somebody (not something) is indeed waiting for us. In the middle of the kitchen, half-hidden by the pile of broken cupboards, a young man is waiting – 20-something, strongly built, dressed in work overalls – and the moment he sees us, his face breaks into a huge smile.

What is this?

We have no time to react, to gauge hostility or friendship, because the young man approaches, hands held out in greeting to the one at our side. They have eyes only for him, not for us. Without a word, they embrace each other and both are weeping and then both are speaking at the same time: 'Thank you for – I am so sorry – I never imagined – you came back – will you let us – free to start – at last.'

Next, to our shock and surprise, we find we are being pulled into the embrace, as if we belonged here, as if we have done something that deserves recognition, instead of simply finding ourselves in a particular place at a particular time. We hear ourselves introduced as a friend; we hear ourselves praised for doing what others could not do.

Our stammering version of what has just happened is waved away (graciously), although the saga of the storm and our castaway status is exclaimed over, and offers of dry clothing and hot soup and general TLC are lavished upon us by the beaming young man – and his friends, who have crowded into the kitchen after him. Similarly dressed in overalls and kitted with heavy-duty boots and gloves, they have come to begin again the work of restoring house and garden which (so we are told) was halted before some of them were even born, when the attic hermit shut the door and declined any further contact. They are family, it turns out, who have waited for the chance to mend, rebuild, repair, renew – but they knew they had to wait for the invitation, however much they longed to make the necessary start.

Even though the day is drawing to a close, the buoyant enthusiasm of the young people has been unleashed and they are already dragging the dusty piles of shelves and cupboard doors outside and lighting a bonfire. One of them – sister, apparently, to the first young man – has found the house keys and is busy throwing open the doors along the gloomy hall, while others fold back shutters and pull down tattered curtains. Everywhere, golden light is pouring in.

I love the Lord, for he heard my voice; he heard my cry for mercy.
Because he turned his ear to me, I will call on him as long as I live.
The cords of death entangled me, the anguish of the grave came
*   over me;*
I was overcome by distress and sorrow.
Then I called on the name of the Lord: 'Lord, save me!'
The Lord is gracious and righteous; our God is full of compassion.
The Lord protects the unwary; when I was brought low, he saved
*   me.*
Return to your rest, my soul, for the Lord has been good to you.
For you, Lord, have delivered me from death, my eyes from tears,
*   my feet from stumbling,*
that I may walk before the Lord in the land of the living.
I trusted in the Lord when I said, 'I am greatly afflicted';
in my alarm I said, 'Everyone is a liar.'
What shall I return to the Lord for all his goodness to me?
I will lift up the cup of salvation and call on the name of the Lord.

I will fulfil my vows to the Lord in the presence of all his people.
PSALM 116:1–14

As already seen (and as is clear from browsing through the Psalms), this ancient book of hymns and prayers demonstrates a recurring pattern of despair becoming hope becoming deliverance through the saving power of the Lord. Knowing that God is able to save is a spur to calling on him in confidence, even though it does not spare us from being overcome by anguish. It does not save us from stumbling, from tears, from being knotted up in the 'cords of death'. The intensity of the speaker's anguish is shown in the way they felt isolated from others by their situation. For whatever reason (hurt? betrayal?), they reached the point of trusting no one. Even proffered help was waved away because (according to this jaded perspective) it probably came with cynical motive or hidden agenda.

Note, though, the tense of the verb used to describe the condition of isolated mistrust: that was how things used to be, back then. What has remained constant and undeniable is God's compassion, graciousness, and particular protection for the 'unwary' – those, maybe, who were not sufficiently guarded against others who would hurt and betray them. The unwary are 'brought low' as they stumble along, weeping, but the Lord sees. The Lord picks them up, brushes the mud from their clothes and sets them walking on a safe path.

As already seen, though, we reach the point of calling out for salvation only when we admit, honestly, our huge need for rescue. All too often, we prefer to endure the unendurable, tolerate the intolerable, for longer than we should. It is only when we acknowledge our tangled, terminal condition in its shabby entirety that we make the connection that will eventually lead to our release and return to the 'land of the living'. There, we can be 'at rest' in the knowledge that, apart from God, we are fundamentally helpless and hopeless. We cannot sort ourselves out, not really. And once we have learned this lesson thoroughly, we will not forget it. We will (all being well) remember to call first and always on the One who alone can save us.

This return to life, this deliverance, calls forth a further response from the speaker, beyond fulsome thanks. Restored to life, reinstated in the community they had thought lost for ever, they long now for the opportunity to share their story, to demonstrate to anyone and everyone that the Lord has come good for them – and they will come good for the Lord, fulfilling whatever they have pledged by way of gift or act of service or dedication. God's mercy is not earned, but it can certainly be celebrated and also inspire an appropriate response of gratitude, an intention to cultivate a life characterised by a bountiful harvest of goodness.

Once begun, the work of restoration continues until after dark. The bonfire has sunk to a rich, red bed of embers that flare white-hot as a breeze plays over them. The young workers – and the former hermit-one – sit around the warmth, and we sit there too, absorbing the straightforward camaraderie. They joke, laugh, swap stories of jobs done and jobs yet to be done; wine is poured, sausages cooked over the glowing coals. Later still someone produces a guitar and there is singing and more laughter. Lulled by the music, worn out by everything that has happened since leaving (how long ago could it possibly be?) the island of green pastures, we close our eyes, hunched as we are by the fire.

We sleep.

When we wake, we find ourselves tucked under a rather itchy blanket under a pale morning sky. The restoration work is already under way again, but our search for anything resembling a hot shower is brought to an abrupt end by our discovering the cracked and stained fittings from at least two bathrooms dumped in the backyard. It is tempting to join in with the happy band of renovators – but this is not our work, not our life. We know that we do not belong here any more than we belonged on the green island; this place has become the family concern it was meant to be all along, albeit an open and welcoming family concern.

So we say our goodbyes, although the young people are too engrossed in their work to stop for long. We take a stroll around the garden, accompanied by the roar of chainsaws, mowers and strimmers, and bend close to listen to our old attic friend who walks with us. They speak again, to our embarrassment, of how, by an extraordinary coincidence, we were the means of unlocking what had been locked away in them for so long. They also tell us that it is not so very far to the next island, the very island that we had been hoping to reach when the storm caught us. We are told that if we walk on a little way, we will come to a boathouse where we will find a blue rowing boat – a rather creaky boat, in serious need of a coat of paint, but perfectly sound for the short pull across the channel that will take us to our destination.

Part 4

Release

10

Stuck

It's extraordinary how the boiling waves of a day or so earlier have turned to flat, silken calm. The air is still, too, but somehow full of soft life, in contrast to the frozen chill of the other morning. There is no sound except the rattle of the rowlocks as we manoeuvre the old blue boat out on to the water. A couple of our new friends had stopped their work long enough to help ease open the rusting hinges of the boatshed door and now they wave us off, shouting goodbyes before disappearing up the path towards the engrossing renovation project. It's hard not to feel a moment's pang of loneliness – but we tell ourselves, yet again, that we have further to go. We know that our journey has not ended; our pilgrimage is ongoing.

As we bend to the oars again and again, inching our way across the smooth channel, the exertion warms us, and before long the sun is strong enough to make us long to reach the shade under the trees fringing the island that lies ahead, the island (so we hope) of waterfalls and hidden valleys. We can see the lush green leaves already.

Where can we land safely? At first glance, the foliage is impenetrable. Our attempts to nose the boat into the shade result in a bit of awkward tangling with roots jutting into the water. Humming clouds of flies emerge from the lush green leaves and insinuate themselves into nose, eyes, ears. At last, a channel opens on our left, dark and overhung but leading inland until the water becomes almost too shallow for oars. Finally, by grabbing on to trailing bushes and hauling the boat as far as it will go, we run aground on a strip of gravelly sand. Here is a hint of path, perhaps just an animal track, but we can follow it, stooping, away from the water's edge and into – what?

Into adventure, perhaps.

The air of this island vibrates with possibility, with energy, as if the massed greenery hides a whole menagerie of living things, besides the humming insects. Sweat starts to trickle between the shoulder blades as we force a way along the narrow track. Gradually the bushes draw further apart. Gradually the trunks lengthen and thicken and become trees. Gradually our hampered progress becomes a saunter down a grassy lane, beneath a cobalt sky dotted with clouds, which can just be glimpsed through the interlacing branches. Although the island is thickly wooded, we can sense its shape as the lane twists and descends, and corkscrews round a curve of rock. Then it plunges suddenly down again along a ridge and into a valley. Even here, in the dense shade, the sunlight dazzles briefly as the wind stirs the leaves and casts dancing shadows on head, hands and feet.

Around us, down the steep valley sides, small waterfalls tumble and splash, sometimes hidden in ferns, sometimes flowing right across our way, challenging us to take a leap or risk a soggy step or two. Below, on the valley floor, we can hear a river running swiftly, although as yet it is out of sight.

This is adventure.

We grow bolder. Steps turn to strides, which turn to bounds, which become running along the hairpin, corkscrew lane that, by this point in its descent, is growing more vertiginous – more (not that we want to admit it, in our adventurous mood) dangerous. But after so many narrow escapes and lucky breaks, our confidence is high. Something will turn up – it always does – as we charge heedlessly into the heart of this island. Even if we can't find shelter or refreshment (other than the water – there is no shortage of water), it's not so very far back to the other island where food and friendship looked to be unlimited.

Here is adventure – go for it.

When we finish our descent to the river's edge, we see an enticing pool on the far side, shaped by the eddying of the water in times of flood. What better place for a dip, when there was no chance of a shower earlier? And because it's adventure and because we are going for it, we don't give a second glance upriver. We don't see the rope bridge (precarious enough but still offering a crossing in relative safety).

Because it's adventure – and we're going for it – we choose instead to jump to reach the pool. We won't attempt the whole river in one go (that would be truly stupid). We will leap from slippery boulder to slippery boulder, exhilaration growing with every wobble corrected, until we come to the leap that will carry us safely over the last stretch of water to dip ourselves in the dark, reed-fringed pool.

A run-up, a jump, a soar through the air – and there is a horrible, heavy landing. Not into clear water, not even on to a joint-jolting rock – but into glutinous, stinking mud. As we gasp and kick out, the quagmire quakes, shifts, quivers… and, inexorably, we feel that we are beginning to sink.

This is no ordinary riverbed layer of mud; this is an illusion of ground, which is in fact a thin layer over an abyss, and now that we have awoken its secret currents, it is on the move. We are trapped over the knees almost before we realise what is happening. Trying to wrestle free turns the breath to snatched mouthfuls – and makes no difference. The mud is inching towards our hips now, while the water laps around our chest.

Ribs are hollow as lungs work hard to suck in air, as if oxygen can be stored for a more convenient time. What a ridiculous, humiliating end this would be: drowned – but in such a shallow river. Floundering, filthy, forgotten, perhaps a line of mud-bubbles left to mark the last gasp – but who will come by to notice?

Deeper – and a little deeper until the mud fits firmly just below the diaphragm. The water teases our lower lips. Then the downward progress stalls… stops… but we dare not try to wriggle free, in case we set the descent in motion again.

We are stuck fast.

The river flows on regardless. The wind stirs the treetops. Flies form a buzzing cloud around our head, but we dare not move to swat them. Don't think about the coming night – it is hours away, as yet – but time is passing, as is clear from the changing shadows and the growing ache in our trapped limbs.

This can't be the end – can it?

As this thought forms, we look up and there, on the bridge just upriver, stands a man, looking back at us.

Out of the depths I cry to you, Lord;
Lord, hear my voice.
Let your ears be attentive to my cry for mercy.
If you, Lord, kept a record of sins,
Lord, who could stand?
But with you there is forgiveness,
so that we can, with reverence, serve you.
I wait for the Lord, my whole being waits,
and in his word I put my hope.
I wait for the Lord, more than watchmen wait for the morning,
more than watchmen wait for the morning.

Israel, put your hope in the Lord,
for with the Lord is unfailing love
and with him is full redemption.
He himself will redeem Israel from all their sins.
PSALM 130

This is prayer as distress flare, sent up in the knowledge that there is no one who can help and no time (or option) for special pleading, self-justification or blame of others (no citing of unspecified 'enemies' here). The one who calls does so 'out of the depths', and the Latin phrase *de profundis* (famously used by Oscar Wilde as the title for his long prison letter to his former lover) arguably sounds even more plangent, the heavy syllables and forcible central vowel pushing us ever deeper down. As with some of the other psalms we have pondered here, the Lord has not yet answered, has not yet delivered, even by the end. The talk is only of waiting and hoping and crying for mercy – and the hours of darkness feel never-ending.

Here speaks one who, perhaps, knows that they have descended to the depths through their own frailty and fault. They remind the Lord (as if the Lord needed reminding) that mercy is the name of the game, that sins are supposed to be forgiven rather than added to an eternal tally, that the relational dynamic is, thankfully, unfailing love, not unmitigated condemnation. It is the Lord's nature to be merciful, forgiving and loving – isn't it? Thus the speaker reflects with (we can surmise) a twinge of understandable anxiety: I cry out, I wait, and I hope – because it's you, Lord, you and no other heavenly or earthly authority, whom I summon for rescue, shooting up my distress-flare prayer from the depths. None other has the power to save one such as I; none other has the grace to be willing to save one such as I.

If we are not careful, talk of 'sin' and 'forgiveness' can lose their force. Rather than acknowledging guilt ('I chose this path because I am weak-willed and selfish'), we may opt for a more congenial narrative, of victimhood for example ('my parents didn't affirm me; my boss bullied me; my partner doesn't understand me – and so this is where I have ended up'). It is important to work at understanding our motives and the desires (which may be hidden even from ourselves) that drive our actions, but sooner or later, walking the path to wisdom and maturity means admitting that sometimes, we mess up. We do harm to others – and thus also to ourselves – and we cannot sort things out. We find ourselves 'in the depths'.

We should note, though, the purpose of forgiveness, as identified by our speaker. We are forgiven in order that we may 'serve the Lord'. The healing power of forgiveness – for both forgiven and forgiver – is immeasurable, but the Lord forgives so that we can be restored to right relationship with him, not so that we simply enjoy a fuzzy feel-good glow, for our personal benefit.

Back in the very beginning of everything, so the scriptures tell us, we were spoken into being by the creator's word, shaped in the creator's image, and called to continue the creator's work of shaping our good and beautiful world, which is the creator's gift to us as a home. We serve because such service is part of God's loving purposes for us. It's not a matter of 'getting on', impressing anyone else, nor yet a matter of unhappy obligation. We find our true dignity and worth in the service that is perfect freedom, a mutual giving and receiving of love and honour and cherishing with our Lord himself.

So there, on the bridge, just upriver, stands a man, looking at us. He is close enough for us to see his face, but his expression is unreadable. Does he feel compassion? We hope so. Irritation? That could be understandable, especially if he is the owner of the land round here. Alarm? Not unlikely, given what our appearance must be, stuck here.

For a long moment we hold each other's gaze. Surely our situation is clear? Do we really have to yell out and explain our predicament?

Then the unthinkable seems about to happen – the man turns his head as if to move away, bends as if to pick up whatever load he had been carrying when he caught sight of us.

There is no time to worry whether he is friendly or hostile. We are truly desperate. We are forced to the point of stammering out words that have never come easily, one way and another... words spoken to us no more than a day or so ago, but which we have rarely deigned to use ourselves.

'Help.'

A little louder – his lack of reaction suggests he hasn't heard – 'Help!'

Louder still, voice cracking: 'Help!'

Whimpering, pathetic, croaking with unshed tears: 'Help, please. Please.'

As if mocking the hope of rescue, the mud shivers once again and something shifts far below, and we feel ourselves beginning to inch down so that the water begins to cover our mouth. Further speech is impossible.

And he comes.

Running with long, confident strides, he crosses the bridge, dipping out of sight for a second and then reappearing on our side of the water. In his hand, coiled ready, is a rope.

There are no wasted words but intense focus in his instructions to stay calm, hold on, don't panic, relax if you can. He reaches to tie the rope securely around our ribs and it hurts – but the voice issuing orders is steadying, almost gentle. Helpless, we can only obey and hope no tears fall until they can come in decent privacy.

The pain of the pulling is immense and we can't help but cry out so the water fills our mouth and we choke and splutter. Then, with a deafening squelch, we are free.

11

Freed

He does not want our thanks as such, he says. We trail after him on shaky legs, stinking of mud, groping for the right thing to say and giving up halfway through a succession of clichéd expressions of gratitude. 'Thank you for an escape from death.' Melodramatic but true. 'If you hadn't come by –' Maybe he'd been there all the time and we just hadn't noticed. 'Words fail to express –' Actually, he does not look like someone in great need of our gratitude. He has rescued us, saved us, as matter-of-factly as if that's what he does every day.

When we were freed and had sat and coughed and gasped on the riverbank for a few minutes, he simply said, 'You'd better come with me,' and set off at a steady pace that made no concession to our post-traumatic shakiness. Somehow or other we manage to keep up as (we suspect) he knew we could.

'This way,' he calls over his shoulder, as the path zigzags up a ridge, takes a sharp left and joins another slightly wider way that has the reassuring look of having been made by vehicle wheels. Two stony grooves, grassy strip down the middle, lead us around the curve of the hill. In places, the outer groove is uncomfortably close to the sloping hillside and worn deep enough to merit a four-wheel drive, if not a tractor.

'Not far now.' And there, tucked in a thicket of flowering bushes, we see a wooden lodge, partly raised on stilts so that underneath there is space for a battered truck as well as tidy stacks of tools, hay bales, sacks – and a wire-haired terrier who trots out to meet us, slightly wary but not unwelcoming. A few chickens scratch about, scattering in alarm at our arrival. Our rescuer bounds up the steps that lead to a veranda and throws open the front door, but we hold back, reeking and muddy as we are. Noticing our hesitation, he nods at a tap in the yard. 'I don't mind the dirt – but if you'd rather, you can sort yourself out first.'

After a bit of ineffectual scraping and rubbing and wringing out, the thick black mineral smears become a general grey layer over everything. Right now, there feels little chance of ever being properly clean again.

Filmed, rather than caked, in grime, we creak up the steps and find our rescuer sitting on the veranda, a jug of something pink and clinking with ice cubes on a side table, next to two glasses and a plate of cupcakes.

'Might as well enjoy the sunshine,' he says, indicating a deckchair opposite him. Jutting on its stilts above the treetops, the veranda gives a fine view over the densely wooded valley that falls away ever more steeply on the further side from the one we traversed. The flowering bushes – red, yellow, white – are alive with bees and, in a clearing beyond the lodge, we see three neat hives. Stealing a glance at our rescuer, we note a lined, brown face, suggesting a life spent mostly outdoors. His hands, filling the glasses, are calloused and scarred, the hands of one whose work is making and mending. It turns out that he is not only a beekeeper but a baker and handyman too, providing for those who visit this island as well as the few who live here long-term.

He still hasn't asked us how we ended up stuck in the mud, or how or why we came to be on the island in the first place. Instead, he describes his daily routine of mixing, kneading, rising, baking – and delivering breakfast rolls to the holiday lodges dotted around the hills and valleys. He describes how he goes out again, late morning, to check that all is well with the newcomers, who are nervously tackling back-to-basics lighting and sanitary systems as they commit to a week or two of island life.

'Funny, though, what you stumble across, when you're out and about on your daily business!' His voice is warm, a little teasing.

A pause – our moment, should we choose to take it.

We choose.

Here goes.

Draining the glass of delicious pink juice and consuming a cupcake in three nervous bites, we begin to tell our story.

And, dear reader, you probably want to know all the details of the story now told – the ins and outs, the sins of omission and the sins of commission, and so on and so forth.

Don't you?

The trouble is, dear reader, that at this point the story can become so comfortably specific to one set of experiences that you overlook the fundamental truth: that anybody can mess up. Anybody, however honourable their original intentions, can find themselves at the end of the road, down in the depths, stuck in the mud, backed into a corner, up a certain creek without a paddle – whether literally or metaphorically. However much they meant to live a godly and upright life, anybody can find themselves making choices that betray their inner frailty and faultiness. Sometimes they get away with it, sometimes they manage to keep the show on the road (or at least the semblance of a show) to the bitter end – and sometimes they don't.

The telling of our story takes plenty of time, but our audience – our rescuer, the wire-haired terrier and one curious chicken – betray no signs of impatience. It is only when our final words are lost in an explosion of tears that our rescuer leans forward and speaks. 'Even burdens carried for years can be put down. Remember this: there is no more condemnation if you do so.'

Despite this – or maybe because of it – there are many more tears.

Have mercy on me, O God, according to your unfailing love;
according to your great compassion, blot out my transgressions.
Wash away all my iniquity and cleanse me from my sin.
For I know my transgressions, and my sin is always before me…
Cleanse me with hyssop, and I shall be clean; wash me, and I shall
    be whiter than snow.
Let me hear joy and gladness; let the bones you have crushed
    rejoice.
Hide your face from my sins and blot out all my iniquity.
Create in me a pure heart, O God, and renew a steadfast spirit
    within me.
Do not cast me from your presence or take your Holy Spirit from
    me.
Restore to me the joy of your salvation and grant me a willing
    spirit, to sustain me.
Then I will teach transgressors your ways, so that sinners will turn
    back to you.
PSALM 51:1–3, 7–13

This psalm is well known as being 'of David', in response to the prophet Nathan's visit to him to administer the Lord's stern rebuke. The king had stolen Bathsheba, the wife of Uriah, one of his most loyal soldiers, and he had ensured Uriah's death to cover up the crime. Having recognised his guilt, thanks to Nathan's skilful words (2 Samuel 12:1–14), David expressed true remorse and experienced forgiveness. Even so, he and his family still suffered consequences from his wrongdoing. Repentance and forgiveness set him right before God but could not undo what he had done, could not turn back time to give him a second chance to avert his greedy eyes from another man's wife.

The psalm speaks of 'washing' and 'cleansing' and, we can surmise, might have been spoken or chanted or sung with tears. We speak of 'crying with laughter', or with joy, relief – as well as with fear, anger, shock and sadness, and (as in this psalm) with regret. Apparently, scientific research indicates that tears wept for different reasons have different chemical compositions. There is therefore a verifiable basis for the idea of 'bitter tears' and thus also for the idea that tears shed in heartfelt penitence – letting go of any attempt at self-defence, in complete acceptance of guilt – can help to bring about the cleansing and healing that we long for in our weeping. Such tears can be squeezed from our pain like diamonds, precious jewels shaped in conditions of near-intolerable pressure. We weep – and we begin to be made whole again.

Also, we can surmise, David may have wept with regret that he, national hero, giant-killer, fearless warrior, beloved of God, would for ever be remembered as much for his failings as his feats. His fighting strength, his mighty bones, were 'crushed' by acknowledgement of his oh-so-human weakness. He may have been Israel's greatest king, leader of a nation, founder of a dynasty, but he was also just another testosterone-fuelled bloke.

If forgiveness is to work its full healing power, the burden of failure has to be laid down, along with regrets and wishes for what might have been. Forgiveness must be received with open hands and unbowed back, rather than taken and attempts made to cram it into a back pocket while we carry on weighed down with the rest of our emotional baggage. To become not only clean but 'whiter than snow' requires commitment from the one who needs cleansing, as well as the cleaner. We should remember that in the days before biological powder and 60-degree washing cycles, achieving that level of whiteness would have been arduous and time-consuming.

It is futile and counterproductive to try and hang on to our dignity in an attempt to whitewash the past, to obscure the inkblot of transgression. Once he had been forced to confront what he had done, David did not look for wriggle-room. He told or sang of his guilt in lyrical poetry – and cast himself on the 'unfailing love' and 'great compassion' of the one who had gifted him and called him to leadership in the first place.

As we have seen before, forgiveness and healing are intended for a purpose that encompasses but is not limited to recovering personal well-being. David will recover joy and gladness; he will experience renewed steadfastness of spirit and a newly minted 'pure heart' – but he will do so in order to call others back to the Lord. Speaking of what we have experienced ourselves is often more powerful than repeating what we have heard elsewhere. Second-hand testimony (however dramatic it may be) is almost always trumped by 'I know this to be true because I have seen it with my own eyes' or 'felt it in my own heart'. Our words carry greater conviction when they emerge (at times, white-hot) from the furnace of our own griefs and failures, our personal joys and victories.

The tears have finished, although for a while they felt as if they would flow without any prospect of ending. In the ensuing hush, it seems as if even the quiet sounds of the surrounding hills and valleys are stilled. The bird-calls, insect hum, water falling, wind in the leaves – all are lulled so that when our rescuer speaks again his words reverberate through the whole valley: 'Seeing your mistakes is good. Reflection on what went wrong – how you went wrong – is good. But no amount of going over the past will change the outcomes. It won't make a new, better pattern that absolves us of responsibility.' Despair momentarily clasps us as tight round the ribs as that sucking quagmire – but he is still speaking. 'What you have to do now is lay it down. And leave it laid down, once and for all. Be free.'

Free? Would we even recognise ourselves if freed from everything that we have carried for so long? We've grown used to a certain lopsided way of getting through life, limping along as best we can. What was broken in us mended crookedly, years ago, but this is how we are… and this brokenness, this crookedness, is familiar in its limitation. Dare we risk a fundamental change? The prospect is daunting.

'Don't be frightened, though.' Our rescuer stretches back in his deckchair, eyes closed, speaking almost lazily. 'At first it's no more than a turning around. You decide to head in a different direction – and then it's a step-by-step, day-by-day thing. Then, one day, you look back and you can't believe how far you've come, how strong you've grown for the next bit of the journey.' A pause – and he speaks again, more softly than ever. 'What do you reckon?'

No more than a turning, no more than a facing in a different direction – that is thinkable. More than that, it is doable. With that, though, comes a sudden spurt of positive energy. This – we choose this, because we want to, not because we have finally and utterly given up.

Yes.

'Come on.' He gets to his feet. 'I think you can manage a final stroll before lunch. I want to show you somewhere special.'

12

Cleansed

Stroll, he said, but this has been more of a trek – again. Starting tired, we move beyond tired into a trance of movement, legs working mechanically to follow in the footsteps of the one who climbs on and up as smoothly as if jointed with steel springs. The grassy path here is well maintained, with trimmed banks of bushes and brambles on either side. Every now and then a little clearing holds a bench assembled from split logs. Although we have no chance to sit and enjoy the view, we pass a man and later a man and a woman doing just that. Our rescuer greets them briefly and they smile a vague 'good morning'. No one looks surprised or bothered at the sight of us, trailing behind, mud-coloured.

'Here we are' – at last.

And it is an impressive sight, even on this island that has been captivating us with its unaffected beauty. We have emerged from a screen of slender trees to stand at the edge of a cliff where a cataract rushes over and becomes a waterfall, which flows down into a wide basin of rock, a natural plunge pool.

'It's not bottomless,' says our guide, 'but there's plenty of depth. Enough for a safe jump and splash.'

Really? The cliff is high – not dauntingly but respectably so, and certainly enough to make anyone sensible pause and check and check again, hesitate and draw back, before daring a running leap.

'Trust me – I've done it myself many times. All you have to do is breathe and let go.' He won't stay and watch – or give us a helping push. This is something entirely of our choosing, although choice and us have not had a happy track record. 'Come back for lunch – and some clean clothes.' And he's already disappearing back along the grassy path, whistling.

Just breathe and let go.

We can do that much.

There's no one to see – so clothes are stripped off. There's no one to give us a countdown, so we have to provide our own, stepping back to get a good lift-off and enough clearance to land just beyond the boiling point where cascade hits surface. As before – don't try this at home, kids…

But this is us, here and now. This is us running fast, taking off, flailing for a second at the top of our trajectory before plunging down and in and deep. Thankfully, it is as deep as he promised. The cool water closes over our head, but almost at once, we are bubbling up to air again, bobbing and gasping in the bright dazzle of it all.

The water temperature soon starts to feel comfortable and we paddle and float and dive and return to the sunlit air again and again. After a while we venture into the shock of the downfall, the water pounding head and body until every cell vibrates and skin glows red.

We have never felt cleaner, more oxygenated, more alive.

And we are hungry.

We clamber out on to the warm rocks, shivering a little as we pull on the heap of travel-worn, travel-soiled clothes, and suddenly we hear happy shouts. A group of four, five, six youngsters comes into view, already in swimwear and laden with towels and a beach ball. It's somewhat disconcerting to find this mysterious, almost magical place now thronged with others – and ordinary, cheerful others at that. As we set off towards what we now find we are calling 'home' (noting this with a jolt of pleased surprise), we reflect on the fact that sharing something does not – should not – diminish our own sense of connection with it. Exclusive access does not guarantee enhanced delight and could even result in the opposite: a numbing familiarity because we never have the chance to learn from the reactions – positive or negative – of anybody else.

Although we took scant notice of directions on our way to the waterfall, the path leads unerringly back to our rescuer's lodge – the Baker's House, as the sign on the gate announces. There's no baker here at the moment, though. He must be off on his daily round of repair and reassurance, perhaps with another quick rescue thrown in along the way. Nevertheless, he has left a welcome ready for us: soup simmering on the stove (chicken, by the smell of it) and a bread roll. A scrawled note tells us, 'Cake in the tin, clean clothes on the chair. Back soon.' It just might turn out to be the case that he's done this kind of thing before.

The soup is outstanding – tender meat, flavoursome stock – and our enjoyment of it is undiminished by the sight of what are possibly relatives of the deceased perching on the doorstep and peering inside, in the hope of scraps. Before sitting to eat, we swap our grubby rags for a worn but serviceable T-shirt (a little on the large size) and overalls that are easily rolled up to fit.

Lunch has progressed to a second slice of the fruit cake in the tin by the time the baker is back, shooing the chickens down the steps and slinging a backpack next to the stove.

'So…' He looks at us, clean, reclothed, fed. 'There's work for you here, if you want.'

Work? That's not an offer we expected.

'Plenty to do here, if you like,' he goes on. 'The season's only just underway and the days will get busy. You can help with the baking, of course, but there's cleaning the lodges, welcoming visitors, that kind of thing.'

We feel a little overqualified for such work, but the straightforward tasks sound unexpectedly appealing. He shows us up a ladder on the first-floor landing, to a room that runs the length of the lodge, under the sloping roof, with a window at each end for ventilation. Mattresses are stacked in a corner because this is, he tells us, where they sleep who are happy to work for board and lodging, while the season lasts.

Are we happy with that?

We decide we are happy – and there's no opportunity to reconsider because soup, bread and cake apparently mean that recompense is due this very afternoon. We are dispatched with a bag of sprays and dusters to spruce up the next lodge along the valley, ready for a new batch of holidaymakers.

The law of the Lord is perfect, refreshing the soul.
The statutes of the Lord are trustworthy, making wise the simple.
The precepts of the Lord are right, giving joy to the heart.
The commands of the Lord are radiant, giving light to the eyes.
The fear of the Lord is pure, enduring for ever.
The decrees of the Lord are firm, and all of them are righteous.
They are more precious than gold, than much pure gold;
they are sweeter than honey, than honey from the honeycomb.
By them your servant is warned; in keeping them there is great
*   reward.*

But who can discern their own errors?
Forgive my hidden faults.
Keep your servant also from wilful sins; may they not rule over me.
Then I will be blameless, innocent of great transgression.
May these words of my mouth and this meditation of my heart be
    pleasing in your sight,
Lord, my Rock and my Redeemer.
PSALM 19:7–14

The very cadence of these verses speaks of balance, security, stability, because that is what we can hope for, when we live according to the 'law of the Lord'. We should set aside here any quibbles as to how we apply to contemporary life individual verses of Leviticus (or whatever) – whether or not to eat shellfish, wear polyester cotton or do whatever is the modern-day equivalent of muzzling oxen while they are treading grain. The focus here is the law as a whole, the concept of God's way as a structure for our lives, a structure intended not to stifle but to refresh, to bring joy, wisdom, light. The psalmist (cited again as David) acknowledges the futility of trying to identify our own wrongdoing, as Jesus spoke centuries later of how easily we nail others' failings, while remaining blind to our own huge flaws (Matthew 7:3–5).

In the light of God's law, however, we can see more clearly. We receive due warning of our weaknesses and also safeguarding against the risks of 'great transgression'. If we seek the way of the Lord, we submit to the rule of justice, mercy and love, not the rule of our wayward impulses and selfish desires. Submitting to the discipline of divine law blesses us (even if we do not feel thus blessed at the time) with treasure – heavenly riches, finer than the purest earthly gold. We are blessed with a sweetness of life that surpasses the sweetest food imaginable.

If we flatter ourselves that, by and large, we can get by on our own wits, make a good fist of life on our own terms, we may indeed find that circumstances turn out OK for us, the gambles paying off, the secret faults staying secret. On the other hand, a single event (chance encounter, random error or whatever) can set off a chain of calamity. Our carefully constructed coping mechanisms unravel as we watch, helpless. Life falls apart, even as we try desperately to hold it together. The trouble with secret faults is that they can weaken the foundations on which we build all that we are – our relationships, responsibilities, ambitions, even faith itself. Like metal fatigue or dry rot, the secret faults work away until we realise, too late, quite how vulnerable we are.

That is what King David was forced to realise by the prophet Nathan, as we saw in the previous chapter. This other psalm 'of David' holds steady to what the speaker knows, for sure, to be true. Following the law of the Lord, tasting its sweetness, revelling in its light, is not just a matter of truth but also of safety. Following that way ensures that those secret faults cannot stay secret. The strong, clear radiance of God shines on them and we see the work we have to do. This work may be arduous beyond expectation; it may involve ridding ourselves of habits and strategies that are so ingrained in us as to be second nature. There is no alternative, though, however much we would like there to be.

Time passes.

Time passes sweetly, hour by busy hour, day by fruitful day, in a manner long unfamiliar to us. The baker – our boss, now – is a kind-hearted yet still exacting master. He does not excuse idleness or sloppy work but is generous with praise for tasks completed to what he deems a good standard.

Each morning, we go from lodge to lodge, delivering the bread, noting whether or not all is well. Visitors come to the island for a host of reasons: to seek peace, to rediscover happy memories of past holidays, to celebrate a special moment in their lives, or to escape something or someone. We understand about that – and understand, too, that a smile can be enough to help them keep their fears at bay until they are strong enough to begin to deal with them.

Others have come to live out their days here and some of these people also want bread, smiles and occasional conversation about friendly, inconsequential matters. There are those who open their door only to the baker, the boss himself, but he will not disclose their reasons for this. We have to be content with speculating in the light of our own experiences and the little we glean from more talkative residents.

We have our own special role for the season, too: the checking and mending of the many wooden bridges that criss-cross the wider streams and rivers of this watery island. Having been shown the weaknesses to watch for and equipped with the right tools, we go about hammering and screwing and adjusting so that nobody finds themselves cut off, perhaps when they need help most. Maintaining bridges is a useful life-skill, truth be told.

When the day's work is done, we often return to the waterfall pool which we have discovered faces west, so that at sunset the waters can flare scarlet and gold. We bathe and are cleansed, again and again. We lie floating, basking in the last of the sunlight, listening to the steady roar of the many waters that converge and pour, so endlessly, from on high.

Time passes – and passes sweetly.

Part 5

Return

13

On the rock

Summer's end has come at last and even the lush green leaves of the island are starting to look tired and faded. The last of the visiting families are heading home for the new school year, regretfully, for this summer has been as good as summers remembered from years past – just the right balance of heat and breeze, sun and rain, so that barbecues can continue as planned but the flowers don't droop and die before their time. We have worked hard and have some small scars on hands and arms to prove it. Now we rest, according to recently established tradition, in the growing cool of early evening, eating a ginger biscuit baked this morning, drinking tea, as the bees catch some late pollen in the surrounding bushes.

Time has passed so sweetly that we don't want to think of what might come next.

The baker – the boss man – says nothing. He doesn't need to say anything. We know, and we know that he knows that we know, that a moment of decision will come soon. We are mindful of other, metaphorical, bridges that have to be repaired, and other, metaphorical, dwellings that need a cleaning that brings new meaning to the word 'thorough'. We know that somewhere – not here, but not so very far away – there is a big pile of metaphorical rubbish that is our responsibility to sort, rubbish that has been left to fester long enough.

The moment has not come yet, though. Not just yet. Right now, in the growing cool of early evening, we sense enough strength left after the day's work for some rest and recreation, an excursion (we decide) to the highest part of the island which visitors like to call 'the mountaintop'. We have climbed up there before, more than once, but something nags at us to go now, at this cool evening hour, and remind ourselves of what lies beyond.

We know the shortcuts to the top, after these months of sweet time on the island. Legs toned with a summer's walking from lodge to lodge, we climb steadily. As we move higher, the trees thin out and grow more stunted, caught as they are by the salt-laced sea wind, and before long we have left behind every bit of lush greenery and are out on to bare, stony turf.

Higher and higher still – one final push – and here we are, on the roof of this world, almost grazing the fat white clouds that laze in the breeze. Look one way and see unbroken blue (apart from a handful of white tops breaking over a reef), sea and sky curving to meet at the far horizon. Look the other way and see – so much nearer than it feels – the land we left, what feels like unimaginably long ago. From up here we can glimpse sandy beaches and hill after hill after green hill, rising one behind the other.

Turning to one side, we see, far below, the island jetty and the shed where the dinghies are stored. Among the baker's other skills is sailing and he is a patient teacher of the clumsily enthusiastic novices who want to venture out to catch wind and wave as part of their holiday excitement. The evening has brought enough breeze for a final tack or two around the little bay on this side of the island and we can see a cluster of red sails that offer a pleasing contrast with the indigo water. We too have learned a bit of sailing, so that we can manoeuvre one of those boats out and about, when the weather is relatively calm. With the baker on board for reassurance, we even made it as far as what we know positively to be the island of our friend, the honky-tonk woman. Strangely (or maybe not), of the cottage and honky-tonk piano and our hostess herself, there is not a single sign.

Did we dream our encounter?

Surely not – but our dreams have changed too, in this happy space of summer. One night we did return in sleep to that sad, decayed bathroom but found it transformed, sparkling, newly tiled, hung with colourful shower curtains and mirrors artfully framed with driftwood. It was as if the energetic renovators of that other desolate island house had broken into our sleeping world and made everything new. As for that other place, we made a return visit to find the garden immaculately pruned, the paintwork refreshed and the door firmly locked. A 'To Let' sign was posted in a downstairs window. We sensed no trace of sadness there, but simply an absence, an air of business rightly concluded.

Standing on the mountain now, we feel joy and peace upwelling within. We are surrounded by sea, yet the rock beneath our feet reaches far deeper than that, so that we are safe, feet secure on the most solid of ground. In that safety and security, in that joy and peace, we can dare to dream of new possibilities.

What if – the thought, the dream, forms slowly – what if we set out again? What if we took the baker with us and set sail into the blue, if only for a season? What might we find there? What might we venture, strengthened by his camaraderie? Could we win him over to come with us? For a heartbeat or two we enjoy that unlikely idea – and then, with a sigh, put it aside. What we cannot put aside is the quiet, nagging, internal something that called us to come up here and that needles away now, in the middle of the peace and joy, telling us that very shortly, we will have a choice to make, a choice about what comes next.

God is our refuge and strength, an ever-present help in trouble.
Therefore we will not fear, though the earth give way
and the mountains fall into the heart of the sea,
though its waters roar and foam and the mountains quake with
their surging.
There is a river whose streams make glad the city of God,
the holy place where the Most High dwells.
God is within her, she will not fall; God will help her at break of day.
Nations are in uproar, kingdoms fall;
he lifts his voice, the earth melts.
The Lord Almighty is with us; the God of Jacob is our fortress…
He says, 'Be still, and know that I am God;
I will be exalted among the nations, I will be exalted in the earth.'
PSALM 46:1–7, 10

What is more durable on this earth than rock? We can quibble about the differing durability of different types of rocks, but when everything else is stripped from a planet – animal life, plant life, water, the very atmosphere – what is usually left is rock, crags, cliffs, ravines, caves, gullies and mountain summits. Yet even the rock changes over aeons of geological time – and sometimes unbelievably fast in the grind and snap of an earthquake. Then, even if we had assumed we were standing firm, feet planted on the strong bones of the earth, we may see the ground groan open before us. We may stagger and fall as rock becomes weak as jelly.

The psalm describes scene after scene of catastrophe – mountains crashing into the waves, tsunamis surging in to reduce the land to rubble. Not only is there natural disaster but political turmoil too, as civil war rages, and powers and dominions are crushed to dust. Terror and dread crowd in from every possible side.

Yet, says the psalmist, we will not fear. Even though national security and stability have gone, even though our planetary home looks to be falling apart, we will not fear, we will not give in to the howling winds of terror.

How can we not?

Because, says the psalmist, we have an unfailing hope – more than a hope, in fact. We have the Lord Almighty. His home is never shaken because his strength keeps it strong, as if its foundations are built on his everlasting shoulders. The streams and rivers there 'make glad' his city, rather than bringing destruction.

This holy city is our home, too.

We are not left at the locked gates, begging the silent watchers on high walls to let us in, please. The wonder of it is this: not only is the holy city the Lord's dwelling-place, but he is also that stronghold himself. He is our fortress and he gathers us into himself for safekeeping. And we're not talking about any old deity – this is the 'God of Jacob', God who makes eternal covenant with his people, even when they are as tricky and unreliable as Jacob, son of Isaac. We're talking about a God who keeps his word, for blessing as well as for judgement. This is the God who is our refuge, our strength, our hope. He simply has to lift his voice for the earth itself to melt. This Lord, the Lord Almighty, is with us and so we can be at peace. We can be still, despite the severity of the personal or national (or meteorological) storm that we are weathering.

Standing on the rock of God, rock that will never be thrown down or torn apart, we can look out over life before, life now and life to come. Standing on the rock of God, strong in his tireless strength, we can grow brave enough ourselves to see clearly what we have done and therefore what we need to do next. We can dream dreams that are not escapist fantasies but the breaking in of new possibilities that we never dared envisage before. We may see trouble approaching; we may gasp in pain as anguish claws at our hearts; and yet we can still rest in God's strength. Even if the weight of what we endure forces us to our knees, we should remember that we are still kneeling on the rock of God and there is no safer place.

The evening breeze has dwindled to a breath and the dinghies are pulled ashore, sails furled. In the stillness, the quiet nagging something (is it instinct? or conscience?) stirs within and, like car headlamps switched to full beam on a moonless night, shows us a way ahead. It is not the only way – we know that. We know so clearly that consciousness generates choices and we are freer than we realise to choose between those choices. We can decide whether we choose for selfish or selfless reasons, with clear eyes or clouded vision, for the good or the harm of ourselves and those whom we say we love.

In this long, golden, late summer twilight, the way lit up before us is the way of return, going back to where we started. Time cannot be wound back, so we don't have to relearn the painful lessons learned as we made the journey here. We have learned about our frailty and limitations; we have discovered resilience; we have learned the importance of maintaining and mending bridges.

As twilight fades into gentle night, we see street lights, house lights, shop lights emerging across the bay, twinkling like chains of stars. Instead of retracing the whole of our previous, soul-sapping journey, we can take the sea road, sailing straight across to that further shore where the stars cluster most brightly. With a steady wind, a favourable tide and calm waters, it should be a manageable crossing even for us, newly competent in sailing (although – once again – don't try this at home, kids, and certainly don't think of trying it alone).

Before night has fully settled in, we make our way down from the top and back along the paths leading to the baker's lodge, the place we have called 'home' long enough for it to have become a comfortable habit. He has been reviewing his logbook of jobs completed and jobs to do – the list never grows any shorter. We enter; he looks at us; he knows that we have chosen.

He smiles.

'You're right,' he says gently. 'It's time for you to go, time for the onward journey. Get the calendar and let's set a date.'

14

Crossing the bay

The autumn equinox is the date we pick, when day and night, light and dark, are in balance before the year turns towards winter and the solstice. Meanwhile we keep busy, working through the boss's 'to do' list as the lodges empty and some long-term residents show signs of going south for the winter, as if following the migrating birds. We are required to close down the empty properties until spring, checking the gutters, draining the water, making sure the cupboards are empty.

One mid-September mid-morning we throw open the front door of a lodge in the heart of the most secluded valley and find unexpected guests, two of them, matted hair protruding from a heap of lodge bedding. They are a burned-out, washed-up couple – a young man and younger woman – scrambling to their dirty feet and stammering out a story that sounds suspiciously rehearsed. They claim dereliction, begging (too swiftly in our opinion) for whatever help might be available. They haven't exactly trashed the place but they have clearly lived there more than a few days, creating a level of mess that erodes any residue of sympathy we had for their predicament.

We load them into the back of the truck, next to the wire-haired terrier who surveys them dourly. Back at the boss's house, we present our findings with a certain amount of eye-rolling and sighing.

But he accepts them; no questions asked.

We are outraged, especially when he invites them to choose mattresses to lay on the attic floor, not far from ours. Then he offers them soup and rolls. Before he can think of showing them the way to the waterfall pool, we draw him aside and voice our disquiet at this easy hospitality.

'I don't see the problem.' His voice is easy too, unthreatened by our thinly veiled criticism. We're cross that we can't hoard the generosity for our exclusive enjoyment. We're anxious that we might have to be as generous to others. We tell ourselves that we want to protect the baker from the unscrupulous, from the endlessly needy – but that is only a small part of the truth. The whole of the truth is this: we are greedy; we like the status of being staff; we don't want to share; we don't want to welcome anyone else into the place we've come to call home.

'But I will want help after you've moved on.' He's right, of course, but knowing what's right and accepting it graciously are two different matters. We are sure that we are trying hard – knots of irritation in the stomach remind us that we are at least trying – yet as our final days pass, so fast, we find that each day is soured by our jealousy.

We have more to learn, certainly. We have to learn to reach out to others, as so many reached out to us in the course of our journeying. Grace received has to become grace extended, in order that the cycle of blessing and healing can continue.

We sense the baker's wry amusement at our feeble attempts to smile at the newcomers. He nods slightly in approval when he hears us choke out a complimentary word or two at their faltering efforts at baking, cleaning out a fridge, or chopping firewood. He doesn't have to spell out the irony of our attitude, given our history. It would be so much easier to be nice if they were a nicer, less lazy, less whining couple. But there it is: we can't hope to pick and choose all the challenges we face, the lessons we need to absorb.

Then our final week is upon us. So many tasks will be left half-finished and will require careful handing over to the (as we privately call them) hopeless newbies. We begin the round of last things: last walk up the mountain, last leap down the waterfall, last nail banged into a wobbly bridge, last bread delivery round.

The last evening comes. The baker prepares chicken stew. 'In memory of a short but happy hen life' is his comment, but the female hopeless newbie has turned vegetarian and restricts herself to a plate of green beans and potatoes, which she toys with, moodily.

How tiresome.

There are no lyrical speeches of farewell, although the male hopeless newbie becomes quite tearful as he describes our 'life-saving intervention'; how he, for one, feels 'back from the dead' because of our discovery of them huddled in that empty lodge. We are somewhat humbled – the newbie's words will be something to turn over and ponder in the days ahead. Perhaps the hopeless pair may, given a bit more discipline and graft, turn out to be not quite so hopeless.

The last sleep is sounder than we expected, given the persistent snoring and sighing of our fellow sleepers.

The last breakfast is a rush of rolls and coffee and ensuring that we're ready to catch the tide at the best hour. Standing on the jetty, loading our three plastic bags of worldly goods (which is three more than we arrived with), we wonder if it's too late to change our mind. We're happy to over-winter, you know. There's nothing and no one expecting us, so no harm in staying a bit longer.

Please?

The words remain unspoken.

What about the dinghy? The baker hands us a business card: 'Leave it on the beach and call this number to say it's there. They're expecting to hear from you.'

Call? How?

He hands us something small and rectangular, folded in newspaper in lieu of gift wrap. 'For you – with thanks – and so you can keep in touch.' It's a mobile phone, not one designed to impress but entirely functional. 'It's got enough credit to get you on your way.'

We exchange hugs all round and the three of them wade in to push us off. One hand on the tiller, with the other we let out the sail – and just before the wind fills it, we snatch a last glance back. The three of them stand together and any inner bleat of jealousy is silenced by the sight of the radiant faces of the no-longer-so-hopeless newbies. They are finding the peace and safety that brought us to this point of new departure. We cannot begrudge them that.

The red sail bellies out and we start to cross the bay.

I say to the Lord, 'You are my Lord; apart from you I have no good thing'…
Lord, you alone are my portion and my cup; you make my lot secure.
The boundary lines have fallen for me in pleasant places;
surely I have a delightful inheritance.
I will praise the Lord, who counsels me; even at night my heart instructs me.
I keep my eyes always on the Lord.
With him at my right hand, I shall not be shaken.
Therefore my heart is glad and my tongue rejoices;
my body also will rest secure, because you will not abandon me to

the realm of the dead,
nor will you let your faithful one see decay.
You make known to me the path of life;
you will fill me with joy in your presence, with eternal pleasures at
*   your right hand.*
PSALM 16:2, 5–11

Once again we hear, we are told, from King David himself. Here he is delighting in what the Lord has given him – the 'pleasant places' allotted to him by life (or heaven's) 'boundary lines', the blessings that he has received from God, blessings that encompass God himself. The Lord has not simply given 'portion' and 'cup'; the Lord is his portion, his cup. Thus the psalmist can say, with sure confidence, that apart from the Lord, he has 'no good thing'.

This abundance of gladness, joy and security must never be treated lightly, never taken for granted. It is a consequence of vigilance, watchfulness and constant awareness of the need for the Lord's counsel. Yes, the path of life has been made clear; yes, there is hope of 'eternal pleasures' to come, but that is not an excuse for complacency, for forgetfulness of the true source of said pleasures. 'It is you, Lord,' cries David, 'you alone who teaches me wisdom so that my own heart in turn can instruct me. If I'm left to my own devices, you will see me stumble and fall, disastrously.'

This is not an argument for nursing worry, for continual anxious checking that we are 'doing the right thing'. We are called not to worry, not to fear, but to trust, to be steadfast and full of a proper confidence that is grounded in God alone.

The confidence extends even beyond death, at a time when the general idea of 'hereafter' was *Sheol*, a shadowy, sombre region that was the destination of the dead. *Sheol* was feared as a place of eternal exile from God's presence. 'Yet,' sings David, 'I believe – no, I know for sure – that the one I trust will not abandon me even when the last breath has left my body.' Eternal death and decay have no part within the boundary lines set by the Lord who is the source of life.

We should always, rightfully, acknowledge that God is not only the giver of life but the giver of life's blessings. We should ask him how we can live with wisdom the life he has given us, how we can handle wisely the blessings he has bestowed on us. We acquire strength emotional and physical, knowledge and insight from our experiences, and a degree of material prosperity (although, for many, never as much as they would like). Strength, knowledge, insight, prosperity – the Bible teaches us that these all come from God's hand.

If we remember to look to him, to keep close to him, we will know ultimate security. And, reassuringly, that means security not only for today but also for every tomorrow to come, no matter what they bring. As we stride the 'path of life' on strengthening legs, mindful of 'eternal pleasures' somewhere far ahead, we should not be caught entirely off-balance when the path becomes steep and stony or debilitatingly hot and dusty. Sure, we may be in 'pleasant places' right now, but in this finite sphere nothing endures for ever – not health, not happiness, not success. Just look at Job.

What a relief, then, to be able to relax, secure, in the arms of the eternal, unchanging Lord.

The boat runs cleanly before the steady wind that pushes the water into small, harmless waves that we cut through with a satisfying splash and occasional bit of spray. The sun warms us as the wind cools us, and slowly the island diminishes behind us.

We haven't looked back again. We have no idea if the three still stand on the jetty, watching our progress, no idea if any other boats have bobbed out to nose around the rocks and inlets and, further round the bay, the cliffs where puffins are said to nest. As the distance increases, so our certainty grows that we have chosen rightly. We have tasted stability, security and hours of well-earned rest, and the time has come, for sure, to apply in new contexts what we have learned. New because they are different from where we have been over this past summer, but at the same time we are going to contexts known from what has come to feel like a very far past indeed. In its newspaper wrapping (sealed in a plastic bag for safety) the mobile phone tantalises. It won't be long, surely, before we can pick up a signal from the mainland. No point in trying now, though, not when the sailing is so smooth.

As we come out further into this wide bay, we feel suspended in the blue, between sea and sky, between wind and water, the distant coastline slipping past in a succession of ridges and curves that, from here, are shrouded in haze. Even as we sigh at the inevitable transience of this happy, peaceful space, we see that the happiness and peace have a deeper source than a bright morning on the water. The source of the happiness and peace are found in the purpose that has put us in this here and now, one hand on the tiller, the other adjusting the sails. If we reneged on our purpose, if we bottled our return and swerved on to a different tack, the happiness and peace would slowly but inexorably drain away. We would, in the end, find ourselves washed up, once again, and that wrecking would be as bitter as everything that went before (if not more so).

15

The recovery of joy

The wind has dropped a little now but our journey has been progressing at a reasonable speed. Chances are we'll reach our destination before dark. The sun now stands at the top of the sky, and a sense of inner emptiness pleasingly suggests lunch rather than any more serious, less easily remedied, deficiency.

We've been following the baker's remembered instructions: which bays look as if they offer safe harbour but are in fact rapidly shelving traps; where reefs lie; where to find the rocky outcrop (here, as promised) that is undeserving of even the modified term 'islet', but where we can moor for a lunch and comfort stop.

There is, in fact, a patch of thin grass on top of the rock, but lower down we find more space to stretch out, enjoying sunlight untempered by any breeze, while the dinghy waits patiently, tethered to a medium-sized boulder. We eat rolls, goat's cheese, an apple, drink from a water bottle that we had forgotten to stow in the shade. Never mind.

We enjoy a few more long moments of peace.

From where we lounge, we can see a smart flotilla of yachts – or is it a regatta? – moving picturesquely against the sandy shoreline.

The island is entirely out of sight now.

We have retrieved the phone from its bag, balancing it carefully on a flat ledge. It demands our attention. It's funny to think that, as yet, the only one who knows the number is our former boss. Wouldn't it be easy, wouldn't it be so temptingly easy, to leave it like that? We would press on to our endpoint, deposit the dinghy somewhere and then head off who knows where, anonymous. Wouldn't that prolong our sense of peace?

It's unlikely, to be honest – and being honest is such a newly acquired habit that we don't want to give it up, not just when we've made this promising start. We switch on the phone and spend inevitable minutes fiddling with buttons, settings, network welcome messages – and then we're ready.

Some phone numbers we have by heart, even though at one time we'd planned never to use them again, had hoped to wipe them from memory.

We need to give ourselves some more time, a breathing space to psych ourselves up.

Texts seem a good way forward – sending them to a random handful of individuals, solely on the basis that we can recall their contact details. 'You'll be surprised to get this message out of the blue – but it's a long story. Happy to tell it sometime over a drink or maybe two.' That kind of thing… friendly, inconsequential.

Within a matter of minutes, the replies come pinging back even faster than we'd expected – you? When? Where? What? How? Why? Questions, questions, questions and each question feeling like a giant step of commitment, another huge decision to add to the already huge decision of return.

It's too much, too soon.

We switch the phone off.

Perhaps an hour passes. A seal pops up to bask at what is probably its customary spot and sinks back at the sight of us, affronted.

Staying here is not a long-term option, seal or no seal. We know that. We have to remember the before time – how not making a decision became, in itself, a decision, which usually did not have a happy outcome. Trouble is, giant steps feel overwhelming and no baby steps seem possible, given the situation. The plunge has to be taken and if emotional energy is in short supply, it should be conserved for priorities.

There we are.

Decision made.

We switch the phone on again; we let our eyes glide over a further three texts that have arrived in the meantime – and key in a number that we could have recited in our sleep. There is a pause; a dial tone; a click.

'Hello?'

Hello – again.

It's been a while.

It's the storyteller's privilege to choose what to tell and what not to tell. That conversation shall remain a private one. You may as well know, though, that the outcome is a rendezvous. We have a deadline for our sailing, an endpoint that will also be a meeting point. It's a decision made with intent, not through inertia, and it means that we must get going, hoping that the failing breeze does not leave us becalmed. Bags are re-stowed, sails hauled up, and we're off, back on track and making good headway in the direction of what soon starts resolving itself into rows of colourful houses, a stone church, a beach. We know so well the few streets of slightly faded shops, know the way round to the tiny supermarket, the shabby public toilets, the butcher's shop clinging on to local trade, the three pubs, the karaoke bar.

Closer and closer – even as we more than half wish the wind to drop entirely, the boat to run aground, a monstrous riptide to appear mysteriously and drag us far away. Then we hear a faint splash to one side, then another. A shining blue-black shape appears and disappears again faster than a blink. There it is again, and again on the other side.

Seals?

Porpoises.

Porpoises – a word hard to say aloud and stay entirely morose. It's a family group of some kind – mother and child, maybe? – and they slip in and out of view, alongside us in what feels like playful companionship, until we are close enough to shore to meet the mildly interested glance of a woman walking a fat spaniel along the beach.

The day is ending; the sun has gone behind some clouds; lights are beginning to shine from the shops, cafés and houses. The porpoises have gone. We run the boat aground on the sand, jump out to haul it above the tideline, call the number (according to instruction) of the one who will retrieve it later.

Plastic bags in hand, we will take the so-familiar turnings down the so-familiar streets to a so-familiar sandwich bar (half an hour till closing time). We will drink the cup of tea awaiting us there and eat a cut-price, end-of-the-day sandwich. And we will begin a long-anticipated, long-forestalled conversation with the one who will be waiting for us in that sandwich bar, a conversation that (while necessary) will be about as comfortable as open-heart surgery without benefit of anaesthetic.

*Come, let us sing for joy to the Lord; let us shout aloud to the Rock
of our salvation.*

*Let us come before him with thanksgiving and extol him with
music and song.*

For the Lord is the great God, the great King above all gods.

*In his hand are the depths of the earth, and the mountain peaks
belong to him.*

The sea is his, for he made it; and his hands formed the dry land.

*Come, let us bow down in worship, let us kneel before the Lord our
Maker;*

*for he is our God and we are the people of his pasture, the flock
under his care.*

Today, if only you would hear his voice,

'Do not harden your hearts as you did at Meribah,

*as you did that day at Massah in the wilderness, where your
ancestors tested me;*

they tried me, though they had seen what I did.'

PSALM 95:1–9

Familiar to many as the 'Venite' (from the Latin for the opening word, 'Come'), this is the psalm set as the first canticle in the Anglican service of Morning Prayer. The full text (most of which is included here) marks an abrupt mood change when the Lord speaks. After lyrical declarations of praise and repeated summons to worship, God responds with an unexpected telling-off. Apparently indifferent to the many complimentary words, God reminds his people of how they risk failing even as their forefathers failed long ago.

The decades in the wilderness, when God made his covenant with Israel and gave them the law through Moses, were also decades of repeated struggle and failure. They were decades of repentance and forgiveness too, but again and again, God's people hardened their hearts. They disbelieved their experience and the evidence of their own eyes and set out to test the Lord, to prove that he loved them, cared for them, as much as he said he did. In consequence, those same disbelieving forefathers and mothers were banned from entering the land promised to them. They were condemned to tramp around the desert until the last one of them died. They had used God's covenant love as a cynical bargaining ploy, rather than holding on to it in trust.

It is so depressingly easy to forget such warning history. It is so depressingly easy – it can feel so glowingly righteous – to get caught up in rapturous worship, in the words, the music, the holy atmosphere, that we forget. We forget the story of those men and women who walked by cloud and fire through the wilderness, saw the Red Sea parted, tasted manna from heaven and water from the rock, yet still hardened their hearts and put their Lord to the test.

If they did, so could we.

How can we help ourselves? How can we not fall into the same trap?

We have to remember. We have to retell the stories of what God has done for us, individually and collectively. We have to recount the stories in scripture of how God has acted in the past, since the very beginning, and remind ourselves of his promises that one day he will act to disclose the full glory of his kingdom so that none can deny it. We must not only retell the stories that we know, but we must also listen to what others have to share too. If necessary, we must adjust our own assumptions and expectations of how God chooses to be at work – and what his priorities are.

And we must continue to praise and worship the rock of our salvation, incarnate to us in the Son, in Jesus. We must rejoice in the earth, the sea and the mountains that he has shaped for us and blessed to us as our home, our dear planet that calls for our nurture and tender stewardship. Even as we struggle to care for what we have been given, so we are privileged with the good shepherd's unfailing, cherishing protection. We are safe in his pasture, guarded in his flock, enfolded in his unceasing love, now and always, for ever.

But remember – be sure to remember not to forget.

The desire for happy endings, clear outcomes and logical cause-and-effect scenarios is quite understandable but hard to satisfy. Does an ending cease to be happy or even in any way good if it involves pain and brokenness? Sometimes it can take years – a lifetime – for the goodness in an ending to be evident, despite its being, on balance, the right thing to happen.

And if wrong behaviour remains unpunished because it remains secret, does that matter if the offender has henceforth lived a godly, righteous and sober life? Most would say that society's smooth working involves justice being seen to be done – but what if the mechanism of justice tears apart more lives than it mends? The stories we tell children tend to be reassuringly straightforward, the good guys easily distinguished from the bad guys, no shades except the starkest black and white. Growing to maturity involves a lot of relearning, of reinterpreting, what we may have been taught to see as unequivocally simple.

Recovering joy, though, involves more than following our social codes and conventions. It involves walking with God at our right hand, step by step in the radiant light of his presence. It involves remembering that we have already arrived at our destination – the safety of our Father's house – even as we continue on the pilgrim road that takes us through life.

It involves recollecting the story of where we, humanity, have come from, the state we are in, and where we are going. It involves being prepared to step back from the personal concerns that feel so pressing and to commit ourselves unreservedly to the purposes of God. It will involve, inevitably, acknowledging that the way we see the world is not necessarily the only way. It involves acknowledging that God is infinite – and thus so very much bigger than we realise – and that joy, once discovered, can be multiplied in its sharing.

So – we sit at a table for two in a steamed-up sandwich bar in a down-at-heel seaside town, second cup of tea poured, half-eaten ham and pickle sandwich (on white) set to one side. We have known forgiveness – and know that there is more to come. We have learned enough courage to start rebuilding bridges. Do we know yet whether the recovery of joy is assured?

The realisation is sudden and heart-quickening: no matter the pain we may yet have to face, no matter what the next part of our journey may hold, we have hope for tomorrow. There, right there, is where the recovery of joy can begin.

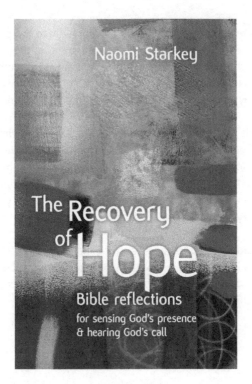

We live in the hope of experiencing first-hand the all-sufficient grace, love and forgiveness which is God's alone, a hope that we may know with our heads long before we feel it in our hearts. This book is centred on a hope that means encountering God not only as consoling presence in the darkness but as one who challenges us to respond to his call. That call may prove to be costly, but as we respond, we will find ourselves transformed as we discover and rediscover not only that we are known exactly as we are, but loved beyond understanding as God's precious children.

The Recovery of Hope
Bible reflections for sensing God's presence and hearing God's call
Naomi Starkey
978 0 85746 417 0 £8.99

brfonline.org.uk

This book is, in some ways, a bit of a mystery tour inspired in part by (although in no way claiming parity with) classic Christian dream texts such as *Pilgrim's Progress*, *Piers Plowman* and *The Great Divorce*, and also by the whole rich tradition of storytelling as a way of exploring aspects of faith and truth. Using story, reflection on Bible passages and quotations for further thought from a range of Christian writers, the trajectory of the book is from emptiness and despair to certain hope, from confusion through penitence to the great joy of forgiving and receiving forgiveness

The Recovery of Love
Walking the way to wholeness
Naomi Starkey
978 0 84101 892 8 £6.99

brfonline.org.uk

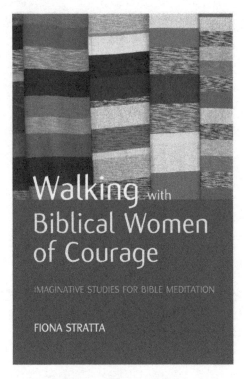

We're all called to everyday courage: the ability to persevere in suffering, resilience in the face of disappointment and loss, strength to take on difficult roles. *Walking with Biblical Women of Courage* is an encouraging and empowering collection of meditative monologues told from the perspectives of women from both the Old and New Testaments. The monologues are followed by questions designed for either individual or group exploration and reflection.

Walking with Biblical Women of Courage
Imaginative studies for Bible meditation
Fiona Stratta
978 0 85746 533 7 £7.99

brfonline.org.uk

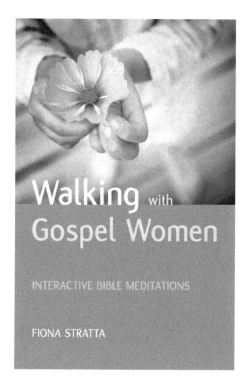

Imaginative meditation can be a powerful way of attuning ourselves to God's presence, involving as it does the emotions as well as the mind. This book offers a refreshing and inspiring way into Bible study, using meditative monologues based around many of the women of the gospels. Through a time of guided reflection, we identify with the woman concerned and see what lessons emerge for today as we ponder her story.

Walking with Gospel Women
Interactive Bible meditations
Fiona Stratta
978 0 85746 010 3 £7.99

brfonline.org.uk

BRF

Transforming
lives and communities

Christian growth and understanding of the Bible

Resourcing individuals, groups and leaders in churches for their own spiritual journey and for their ministry

Church outreach in the local community

Offering three programmes that churches are embracing to great effect as they seek to engage with their local communities and transform lives

Teaching Christianity in primary schools

Working with children and teachers to explore Christianity creatively and confidently

Children's and family ministry

Working with churches and families to explore Christianity creatively and bring the Bible alive

Visit **brf.org.uk** for more information on BRF's work
Review this book on Twitter using **#BRFconnect**

brf.org.uk

The Bible Reading Fellowship (BRF) is a Registered Charity (No. 233280)